I dedicate this book to my wonderful husband that loves my cooking and puts up with me working countless hours every day and to all my family, friends, and clients who inspired me to write this book.

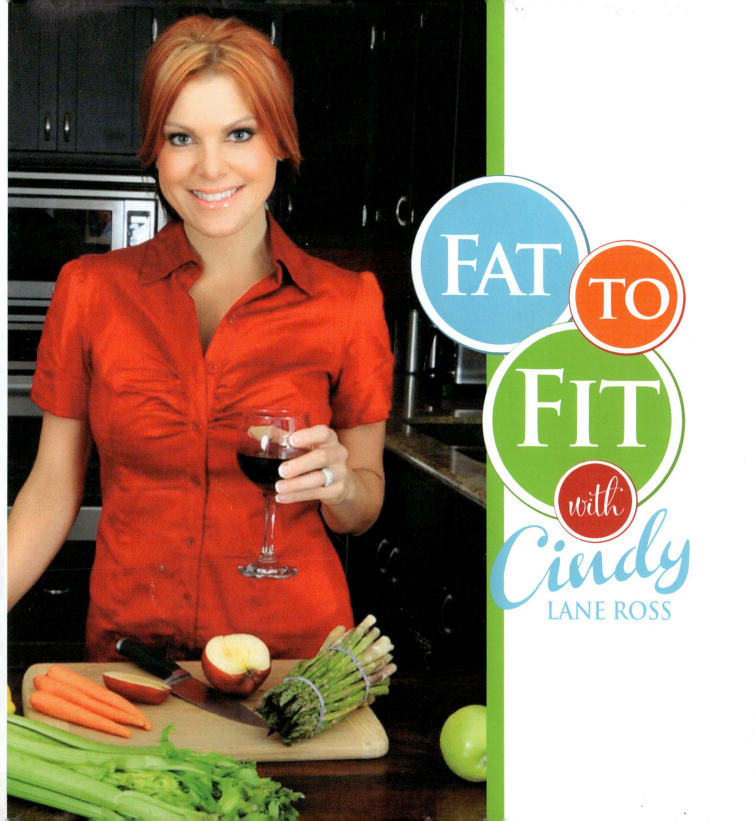

This book is intended as reference only, not as a medical manual.

The information give here is designed to help you make informed decisions about your health.

It is not intended as a substitute for any treatment that may have been prescribed by your doctor.

If you suspect that you have a medical problem, I urge you to seek competent medical help.

Mention of specific companies, organizations, or authorities in this book does not imply endorsement by the author or publisher, nor does mention of specific companies, organizations, or authorities imply that they endorse this book, its author, or the publisher.

Printed in the United States of America

Author - Cindy Lane Ross

Book design by Madalina Calcan
Illustrations by Madalina Calcan

Contents

7 Glossary
9 Cindy's Top 10 Fitness Tips
11 What is Gluten and Are you Gluten sensitive?

13 BREAKFAST

31 The Ideal Grocery List for Good Health
33 Eating a Healthy Diet to Maintain Weight Loss
33 Eating Frequently

35 APPETIZERS

53 Grocery Store Tour
55 The numbers on produce- what does it mean?

57 LUNCH

93 Spicing Up Your Meals When Eating Clean

97 DINNER

169 Healthy Snacks to munch on while sitting at your desk!
170 H2O
171 Healthy Snacks for a Busy Summer

173 DESSERTS

193 Foods to Stay Away From when Eating Clean!
194 Clean Eating Principles
195 Super Greens
196 What does a 1200 calorie day look like?

199 SMOOTHIES AND JUICES

223 Artificial Sweeteners
225 Healthy Cooking Alternatives

229 DRESSING AND SAUCES

247 Berries are Superfoods that can improve your overall health!
248 Benefits of Dark Chocolate
250 Healthy Cooking with Bodies By Cindy
251 Omega 3's and how do you get them from food
253 Lettuce - Which one do we choose and which one is the best for us and why?

Glossary

The Gluten-Free Certification Organization (GFCO) is a program of The Gluten Intolerance Group. The GF logo stands for the independent verification of quality, integrity, and purity of products. Products carrying the GF logo represents unmatched reliability and for meeting strict gluten-free standards. GFCO is the leading gluten-free certification program in the world.

Milk-allergic consumers and the parents of milk-allergic consumers should be somewhat cautious about the use of food products labeled as dairy-free or non-dairy. These terms can appear rather prominently on the labels of food packages. However, these terms should not be used as a short-cut to examination of the ingredient statement that appears on the package label.

Vegetarian food is completely free of all meat, fish, poultry, and other animal products. This includes chicken broth and foods cooked with meat. Many vegetarians also do not include gelatin in their diets, as it is frequently of animal origin.

Cindy's Top 10 Fitness Tips

DECIDE TO MAKE A LIFESTYLE CHANGE - Do not look for a quick fix, when becoming healthier it needs to be a slow progression that is implemented into your daily routin e for long term results.

FIND SOMETHING OR SOMEONE TO BE ACCOUNTABLE TO - If you are having trouble reaching your fitness goals and cannot seem to find the motivation to get back on track then you need to find a program that gives you the reason to eat better and get moving. This accountability can come from a gym membership, a personal trainer, or a group fitness program such as an outdoor boot camp.

START READING LABELS - First you need to learn all you can about the right nutrition, there is an abudance of information online and in magazines. Learn how many calories you need to consume and start reading labels. Check the ingredients list and serving sizes. Portion control is everything!

BUY A SCALE - This is my biggest weight loss tool. Most people who battle their weight find stepping onto a scale frightening, but the scale is your FRIEND! I tell my clients to weigh first thing every morning. It is the tool to keep you on track When you have had too much sodium in your diet, your weight will fluctuate a few pounds. Too much sodium is a culprit and can sabotage your weight loss goals by making you retain fluid.

CHANGE YOUR MENTAL ATTITUDE - When you start giving your body a make-over by incorporating a change in diet and exercise, you also have to change your mind set. People with weight issues must change their perception of food. You must think of FOOD AS FUEL, only eat to feed the body the nutrients and vitamins it needs. I struggled with my weight for many years because of my addiction to food, therefore I had to change my way of thinking.

BE STRONG - There are going to be enablers around you 24/7 trying to wreck your healthy eating habits and your workouts! "Just take a bite, it won't hurt you!" YES IT WILL! or "Skip a workout and lets go grab dinner." THERE WILL ALWAYS BE DINNER AFTER A WORKOUT! Holiday times are the worse, misery loves company and if everyone is eating bad foods and feeling guilty they want you to do the same. You have to refrain and have self-control to make the right choices during these times.

SET REALISTIC GOALS - You did not put the weight on overnight, so don't expect it to come off overnight! Slow and steady wins the race. Make small goals every week and work hard to achieve them.

JOURNAL - There are many online nutrition journals where you can log your food daily or simply take a notebook and keep a daily log. There are even apps on the smart phones for your convenience now. I think you make better choices when you actually write down everything you eat and drink. I feel most people don't realize how quickly the calories add up. This helps you become more aware of what you are putting into your mouth.

GET MOVING - You have to have a good exercise program that is going to keep your heart rate elevated the duration of your workout! My workouts consist 30-45 minutes a day 6-7 times a week of cardio and exercises that consist of using my own body weight or up to 5 lbs dumbbells. With having rheumatoid arthritis, the cardio helps keep my joints nice and loose through the day and the light weight exercises keep my bones strong which helps build muscle tone.

ATTITUDE! - If you don't have this one down, you will not reach any goal that you set for yourself! Your attitude will MAKE OR BREAK YOU! A positive attitude will take you further than you can imagine!

**Put a SMILE on your face, clean out the pantry,
lace up those shoes,
and GET MOVING!**

What is Gluten and Are you Gluten sensitive?

Gluten Free is the new craze, how do you know if it's for you?
More than 55 diseases have been linked to gluten, the protein found in wheat, rye, and barley. It's estimated that 99% of the people who have either gluten intolerance or celiac disease are never diagnosed. It is also estimated that as much as 15% of the US population is gluten intolerant. Could you be one of them?

Six common symptoms of gluten intolerance
(1) Gastrointestinal (GI), stomach, and digestive problems. These can include one or more of the following: gas, bloating, queasiness, abdominal cramping, constipation, diarrhea, or an alternating combination of both – IBS (Irritable Bowel Syndrome).
(2) Headaches and/or migraines.
(3) Diagnosis of an autoimmune disease such as Hashimoto's thyroiditis, rheumatoid arthritis, ulcerative colitis, lupus, psoriasis, scleroderma or multiple sclerosis.
(4) Emotional issues involving chronic irritability and sudden, irrational, mood shifts.
(5) Neurological issues. This may include dizziness, difficulty balancing, and peripheral neuropathy affecting nerves outside the central nervous system and resulting in pain, weakness, tingling or numbness in the extremities.
(6) Fatigue, brain fog, or feeling tired after eating a meal that contains gluten.

Breakfast is the most IMPORTANT meal of the day!

So many clients come to me and wonder what to eat and
I stress this is the most important meal of the day!
Everyone is short on time and this is the meal that always gets skipped.
Breakfast is indeed a very important meal.
A good breakfast fuels you up and gets you ready for the day.
In general, kids and teens who eat breakfast have more energy,
do better in school, and eat healthier throughout the day.
Without breakfast, people can get irritable, restless, and tired.
So make time for breakfast — for you and your kids!

Great picks after Breakfast
Greek Yogurt
Oatmeal
Cereal
Whole Grain Bagel or
rice cake with Peanut butter
Eggs
Smoothies
Fruit
Protein bar

Eating a morning meal is also a healthy habit if you're watching your weight.
Here's why:
research shows that regular breakfast eaters tend to be leaner
and dieters are more successful at losing weight
- and keeping it off - when they eat breakfast.
What's more, people who typically eat breakfast also get more fiber
(more on why this is important later), calcium, vitamins A and C,
riboflavin, zinc and iron - and less fat and dietary cholesterol.
Perhaps it's because they often eat cereal,
which is fortified with vitamins and minerals,
and fruit, which is naturally nutrient-rich.

BREAKFAST

"Success is not final, Failure is not fatal, It is the courage to continue that counts."
Winston Churchill

Yogurt & Muesli Ⓥ

This was a favorite breakfast in Thailand that we brought back and have been enjoying. Muesli is huge in Europe as well! It's healthy and full of flavor

Ingredients

Grain flakes, for example rolled (flaked) oats, wheat flakes, rye flakes etc.
Dried fruit
Nuts and seeds, whole or chopped, to taste
Milk
Yogurt
Fresh fruit, if desired

Basic Muesli Recipe

4 cups rolled (flaked) grain (barley, oats, rice, rye, or spelt)
1/2 cup (65 grams) sunflower seeds (hulled)
1/2 cup (32 grams) pepitas (pumpkin seeds)
1/2 cup (72 grams) sesame seeds
1 cup (95 grams) almonds, roughly chopped
1 cup (230 grams) dried fruit, chopped
1 tsp (2.6 grams) cinnamon, ground
Fresh fruit, to serve
Plain yogurt, to serve

What are the nutritional benefits of muesli?

- Muesli typically has less sugar and calories than most breakfast cereals on supermarket shelves.
- It's high in fiber and whole grains, which regulate the digestive system, are filling and can aid in weight control.
- Muesli is a potent source of antioxidants.
- The addition of nuts provides a great source of protein and omega-3 fatty acids (especially walnuts).
- Milk or dairy alternatives that usually accompany muesli is a source of dairy and protein.

Nutritional Information
- Calories: 150.7
- Fat: 5.8 grams
- Carbohydrates 28.0 grams
- Protein: 7.1grams
- Fiber: 3.7grams

Nut Berry Rice Cake Crunch (GF) (V)
(Cindy's favorite snack)

*This snack is yummy, fast, and will kill your sweet craving!
Its healthy, high in protein and big on taste!*

Ingredients

1 Caramel Corn Rice Cake
2 tablespoons of Greek yogurt
2 strawberries sliced
10-12 Almonds
A pinch of mozzarella cheese
A dash of cinnamon
1 packet of stevia

Directions

Spread the yogurt on top of the rice cake
Layer with sliced strawberries
Top with Mozzarella cheese, almonds, cinnamon, and stevia
No baking required!
Serve and enjoy!

Nutritional Information
- Calories: 188
- Fat: 3.2 grams
- Carbohydrates: 21grams
- Protein: 18 grams
- Fiber: 1.4 grams

Egg White Muffins

Everyone is short on time in the morning, busy lives with work and getting kids off to school. This is a recipe that is simple, can be prepared the night before and the whole family will love them. Easy to throw in the microwave to heat up and eat in the car if you are running late.

Ingredients

1 large carton of all whites- egg whites
1 bellpepper
1 medium onion
2 cups of spinach
1 tbsp of black pepper
1 tsp of sea salt

Directions

Preheat oven to 350.
Spray a muffin pan with spray oil.
Add in your veggies to each cup. 1/3 cup of egg whites per each muffin. Sprinkle your salt & pepper on each one. Place in the oven for 20-25 min. or until you no longer see liquid.
This recipe makes 12 egg muffins.

Nutritional Information
- Calories: 137.9
- Fat: 3.2 grams
- Carbohydrates: 5.4 grams
- Protein: 15.4 grams
- Fiber: 1.2 grams

Sweet Potato Hash Browns

Great For Breakfast!
Sweet potatoes provide sources of beta-carotene and Vitamin A

Ingredients

1/4 cup canola oil
1 red onion, thinly sliced (about 2 cups)
1 green bell pepper, diced (about 2 cups)
2 pounds sweet potatoes, quartered and cut into 1/4-inch slices
1 teaspoon ground cumin
2 teaspoons sea salt
1/2 teaspoon red pepper flakes
1/2 cup green onions, chopped

Directions

Pour the oil into a large skillet and place over high heat. Add the onion and bell pepper and saute, stirring, 2 to 3 minutes. Add the potatoes, cumin, salt and red pepper flakes, lower the heat to medium-high and cook, stirring occasionally, for 25 to 30 minutes, or until the potatoes are fork tender and some are browned. The potatoes will begin to stick as they cook. Just continue to turn with a spatula. Stir in half of the green onions, top with the remainder, and serve immediately.

Nutritional Information
- Calories: 139.8
- Fat: 2.8 grams
- Carbohydrates: 8 grams
- Protein: 0.7 grams
- Fiber: 4.2 grams

Gourmet Caprese Egg Breakfast Sandwich

This Breakfast Sandwich packs a lot of Flavor!
This is one tasty sandwich the whole family will love!

Ingredients

Flat Out - 90 calories
2 Eggs
1 tablespoon of Smart Balance Butter Spread
1/3 cup of spinach
Sun-dried Tomatoes packed in oil
Goat Cheese
Salt & Pepper To taste
Cindy's special sauce

Directions

In a small non stick skillet- melt butter. Drop eggs in, you will cook until the white becomes solid, then flip and cook for an additional 45 seconds. Prepare your sandwich before cooking your eggs. Layout your flat bread, on one end spread Cindy's special sauce. Cut slices of goat cheese and place on top. Sprinkle sun-dried tomatoes on top and then place your spinach. When your eggs are done, place on top and fold over your flat out bread.

Cindy's Special Sauce

Ingredients: 2 tablespoons olive oil, 3 Pepperchinis (Greek Peppers), 1/3 cup feta cheese, 1/3 cup almond milk, 1 teaspoon of sea salt, 1 tablespoon of honey dijon mustard, 1 teaspoon vinegar, 1 teaspoon red wine vinegar, 1 teaspoon fresh basil, 1/2 teaspoon mustard seed, 1 packet of stevia or splenda.
Directions: In a food processor blend together the above ingredients and refrigerate.

Nutritional Information
- *Calories: 166*
- *Fat: 6.7 grams*
- *Carbohydrates: 15.5 grams*
- *Protein: 9.9 grams*
- *Fiber: 2.8 grams*

Cindy's Homemade Gluten Free Pancakes

*Here is a breakfast treat packed with flavor!
Don't feel guilty eating these pancakes since they are Gluten Free*

Ingredients

1 1/2 cup of Bob's Red Mill Gluten Free Flour Mixture
2 1/4 tsp of baking powder
3 tablespoons of baking stevia
2 Eggs separated
1 cup of almond milk
1 cup of blueberries
3/4 tsp of sea salt
3 tablespoons of melted Smart Balance butter spread
Side of honey or pure maple syrup

Directions

In a small bowl, beat egg whites - set aside.
In a separate bowl, sift together flour, baking powder, stevia, and salt.
Beat egg yolks in a medium mixing bowl: add milk and melted butter.
Stir egg mixture into dry ingredients: mix until batter is smooth and stir in blueberries.
Fold in Beaten egg whites. Bake on hot greased griddle over medium heat.
Makes 8-10 pancakes.

Nutritional Information
- Calories: 65.6
- Fat: 1.8 grams
- Carbohydrates: 11.2 grams
- Protein: 2.3 grams
- Fiber: 2.7 grams

Protein Pancakes GF

Ingredients

6 egg whites- beaten until fluffy
1 tbsp of almond milk
1/2 cup of Greek yogurt
1 scoop whey protein powder
1/3 cup of flax seed- milled
1 tbsp of olive oil
1/2 tsp of sea salt
1 tsp baking powder
1/2 tsp cinnamon
1/3 tsp nutmeg
Cooking spray

Directions

Place all ingredients except beaten egg whites in a food processor and pulse or blend until mixture is even. Pour blended ingredients into a bowl and add the egg whites. Mix together. Prepare a griddle with cooking spray. Spoon pancake mixture onto griddle and cook until both sides are lightly browned. Top with fresh sliced strawberries, blueberries, or honey. Makes 6 pancakes. Cooking time: 10 min.

Nutritional Information
- Calories: 48.5
- Fat: 1.7 grams
- Carbohydrates: 5.7 grams
- Protein: 5.1 grams
- Fiber: 3.2 grams

Egg white omelet ⓖⒻ

Ingredients

4 egg whites
2 tbsp of almond milk
6 cherry tomatoes
1 clove garlic
1 handful of spring mix
1 tbsp of purple onion
1/2 tsp of fresh ground pepper
Cooking spray

Nutritional Value:
- *Calories:203*
- *Protein: 20grams*
- *Carbs: 18grams*
- *Fiber: 2grams*
- *Sugars:3 grams*
- *Sodium: 172grams*

1 serving
Cooking time: 5 min.

Directions

Beat eggs with almond milk and black pepper. Sautée vegetables lightly until soft. Pour eggs into small skillet coated with cooking spray. Cook until firm and add vegetables. Fold in half and enjoy. Optional add in mozzarella cheese.

Nutritional Information
- *Calories: 54.9*
- *Fat: 1.2 grams*
- *Carbohydrates: 9.2 grams*
- *Protein: 4.4 grams*
- *Fiber: 0.5*

The Ideal Grocery List for Good Health

PRODUCE & WHOLE FOODS

Fruits – Apples, oranges, bananas, strawberries, cantaloupe, watermelon, cherries, grapes, blueberries, avocado, raspberries, nectarines, peaches, apricots, tomatoes, pineapple, honeydew melon…

Vegetables – Onions, mushrooms, carrots, peppers, zucchini, broccoli, celery, asparagus, beets, cauliflower, spinach, cabbage, squash, cucumbers, romaine lettuce, kale, brussel sprouts, radish…

Beans – black, pinto, kidney, navy, and/or garbonzo. These are easy to toss into the slow cooker or crock pot with a little salt and pepper; buy large bulk bags for the cheapest and lowest sodium options.

Nuts – Almonds, walnuts, pecans etc.

Whole, unprocessed grains
- Quinoa
- Whole wheat pasta
- Steel cut oats
- Couscous
- Brown Rice

Meat
- Chicken Breast
- Ground Turkey
- Fish & Seafood (salmon, halibut, cod etc.)

Dairy
- Low fat milk, Almond Milk, Coconut Milk
- Eggs
- Plain yogurt or Greek yogurt for more protein – This can also be used as sour cream. Pick up some honey to sweeten it if you can't stand the thought of eating plain yogurt.
- Cottage cheese
- Butter – no imitations or zero calorie sprays, you'll just end up hungrier and pumping your body full of chemicals
- Cheese – as little processed as possible; avoid cheese "products", imitation cheeses, or anything that's insanely low calorie as it's probably nutritionally null and void, at best. Goat Cheese and Feta Cheese are great choices.

For flavoring dishes & cooking
- Spices, buy or grow fresh when possible for best taste – cinnamon, oregano, cilantro, black pepper, garlic cloves, cumin, cayenne pepper, ginger, parsley, red pepper flakes, coriander, pure vanilla extract (not imitation) ...
- Pure Honey – Best organic & unpasteurized, great for naturally sweetening things up
- Cooking oils – Sesame oil, vegetable oil, olive oil (do not cook with high heat when using olive oil)...

Other, miscellaneous
- Canned tomatoes
- Nut butters
- Whole wheat wraps & almond flour

Eating a Healthy Diet to Maintain Weight Loss

A knowledge of basic nutrition will help you to make the right choices about the sort of food you eat. A balanced diet contains:
- some protein such as lean meats, fish, chicken, turkey, eggs, soy foods, pulses.
- some carbohydrates such as pasta, rice, bread, potatoes.
- some fats such as oil, nuts and seeds
- some fruits and vegetables.

If you have a healthy balanced diet you should not need to take any extra vitamins or minerals in tablet form. Build some indulgences into your plan. You want a lifestyle diet that works so you need a few sins too.
- Only eat when you are hungry.
- Never eat unless you are hungry. Eating simply out of habit or boredom will not help you to slim.
- Exercise helps. Exercise will burn off calories, keep you fit and keep you toned. It also increases your metabolic rate so makes losing weight easier.
- Reward yourself. When you reach weight goals reward yourself, with an outing or by buying yourself some goodies.
- Don't beat yourself over the head if things go wrong; just re-focus and press on.

Eating Frequently

By eating frequently you achieve the following:
- Eating frequently prevents hunger pangs and curbs over eating.
- Eating more often keeps your metabolism working quickly so you burn calories more efficiently.
- Food is also absorbed more efficiently and quickly when we eat regularly.

APPETIZERS

"You can't out exercise bad nutrition."

"Let exercise be your stress reliever, not food!"

Hummus (GF) (DF) (V)

This is a great staple, can be used as a spread on wraps and sandwiches or
Dips for chips and veggies.
And Hummus is packed with fiber.

Ingredients

¼ cup of tahini
¼ cup of lemon juice
Blend in Processor for 1 minute
Then add 1 clove of garlic-minced
2 tbsp of olive oil
½ teaspoon of ground cumin
½ teaspoon of sea salt
Process for another minute
Scraping sides down
1 can of chick peas- drain and rinse

Directions

Add ½ of can to processor and blend.
Add remaining can. Blend for 1-2 min. Then add 1-2 tbsp of water for extra creamy hummus
Add to plate, drizzle with olive oil and a dash of paprika or Sumac. Using chips, pita bread, or veggies.

Nutritional Information
- Calories: 215.9
- Fat: 12.8 grams
- Carbohydrates: 21.2 grams
- Protein: 5.8 grams
- Fiber: 4.5 grams

Ground Turkey Nachos

Also above dry fajita seasoning, you can use on anything for a powerful taste!

Ingredients

1 pound ground turkey
2 cloves garlic, chopped
freshly ground black pepper to taste
2 teaspoons crushed red pepper flakes
2 tablespoons chopped fresh chives

2 tablespoons hot sauce
1 (14 ounce) can black beans (rinsed)
1 (14.5 ounce) package whole grain tortilla chips
2 cups shredded Mozzarella Cheese
1 ripe tomato, diced
1 jalapeño pepper

My dry fajita seasoning

2 teaspoons chili powder
1 teaspoon sea salt
1/4 teaspoon ground cumin

1 teaspoon paprika
1/4 teaspoon garlic powder
1/2 teaspoon onion powder
1/4 teaspoon cayenne chipotle powder
1 tablespoon of corn starch

Combine all ingredients in a bowl and whisk together- is equivalent to one pre made packet.

Directions

Preheat oven to 350 degrees F(175 degrees C). In a large skillet over medium heat, begin to brown the ground turkey. Stir in garlic, pepper, 1 teaspoon red pepper flakes, and 1 tablespoon chives. Stir in 1 tablespoon hot sauce. When the turkey is browned, stir in fajita seasoning mix. Pour the beans into a microwave safe bowl, and heat in the microwave until softened. Stir in 1 tablespoon chives and 1 tablespoon hot sauce. Spread the whole grain tortilla chips across the bottom of a baking sheet. Spoon the beans mixture over the chips. Then spread the turkey mixture across the top. Sprinkle cheese and remaining 1 teaspoon of crushed red pepper flakes over the top. Top with Diced tomatoes and fresh jalapeño slices. Bake in preheated oven until cheese is melted, about 12-15 min.

Nutritional Information
- *Calories: 295*
- *Fat: 12.3 grams*
- *Carbohydrates: 21.7 grams*
- *Protein: 25.8 grams*
- *Fiber: 1 grams*

Homemade Carrot and Cauliflower Soup (GF) (DF) (V)

This soup is great all year round, healthy and tastes wonderful

Ingredients

1 tablespoon olive oil
1 yellow onion, chopped
5 medium carrots, peeled and coarsely chopped
1/2 head cauliflower, cut into florets
1 teaspoon red pepper flakes
2 teaspoons lemon zest
1 teaspoon ground cumin
2 cups chicken or vegetable stock
3/4 cup plain yogurt, divided
Kosher salt and freshly ground black pepper
1 green onion, finely chopped

Directions

Heat the oil in large pot over medium heat. Add the onions and cook until tender, about 5 minutes. Add the carrots, cauliflower, red pepper flakes, lemon zest, cumin, stock, and 2 cups water and bring to a boil. Cover and simmer over low heat until the carrots are very tender, about 30 to 40 minutes.

Let the soup cool slightly, and then blend until smooth, working in batches. Pour the soup into a large bowl and whisk in 1/2 cup of the yogurt.

Taste and season with salt and pepper. Chill the soup in the refrigerator for at least 2 hours up to 24 hours. Serve the soup in individual bowls with dollops of remaining yogurt, and some chopped green onion.

Nutritional Information
- Calories: 63.4
- Fat: 2.9 grams
- Carbohydrates: 8.4 grams
- Protein: 0.7 grams
- Fiber: 2.5 grams

Black Bean Soup with Turkey Bacon

This appetizer is high in protein and delicious!

Ingredients

- 10 slices Turkey bacon, finely chopped
- 2 medium onions, chopped (about 2 1/2 cups)
- 6 garlic cloves, pressed
- 1 (14 1/2-ounce) can reduced-sodium chicken broth
- 1 1/2 cups canned chopped tomatoes
- 2 tablespoons ketchup
- 2 teaspoons Worcestershire sauce
- 1 tablespoon chili powder
- 4 (15 1/2-ounce) cans black beans, drained but not rinsed
- Kosher salt and freshly ground black pepper
- 1 bunch cilantro
- juice of 1/2 lime
- Thinly sliced scallions, for garnish
- Greek Yogurt, for garnish
- Mozzerella Cheese, for garnish

Directions

Put the bacon into a large heavy pot and place it over medium heat. Cook until it starts to give up its fat, about 4 min. Stir in the onions and cook, stirring, until they start to turn translucent, about 4 minutes. Stir in the garlic and cook until you can smell it, about 1 minute. Add the broth, tomatoes, ketchup, Worcestershire, and chili powder.

Stir in the beans, turn the heat to high and bring to a boil. Adjust the heat so the soup is bubbling gently and cook 10 min. Season with salt and pepper. Meanwhile, pick off all the thick stems from the cilantro. Wash it and shake dry. Chop the cilantro coarsely and stir it into the soup when it has been simmering 10 min.
Cook until the soup is thickened, about 5 min.
Stir in the lime juice. Serve with the garnishes.

Nutritional Information
- Calories: 152.1
- Fat: 2.8 grams
- Carbohydrates: 24.7 grams
- Protein: 8.3 grams
- Fiber: 8.4 grams

Holiday Shrimp Cocktail GF

Great Appetizer for the Holidays that Friends and Family will love!

Ingredients

1 pound of shrimp, peeled and de-veined
2 tablespoons of olive oil
1 teaspoon of sea salt
1 teaspoon of ground black pepper

Sauce Ingredients

1 cup ketchup
1 Lemon juiced
1 teaspoon of Worcestershire sauce
1/2 teaspoon sea salt
1/2 teaspoon fresh ground pepper

Directions

Preheat oven to 400 degrees. On a large cookie sheet, line with foil and spray olive oil to coat. Lay shrimp flat and coat with olive oil. Toss with Sea Salt and Black Pepper. Place in oven for 8-10 minutes, you want a bright pink color.

Don't let the cholesterol in shrimp fool you. *When it comes to heart health, saturated fat is more important than cholesterol - and shrimp is very low in saturated fat. Shrimp is a source of good fat - in the form of omega-3's which helps to reduce triglyceride levels and lower the risk of a heart attack. Although eating shrimp too frequently could slightly raise LDL cholesterol levels, it also increases levels of HDL - the good cholesterol which improves the ratio of good cholesterol to bad cholesterol which is a positive for heart health. The omega-3's found in shrimp also have anti-inflammatory effects which are not only good for the heart, but may reduce the symptoms of diseases such as arthritis.*

Health Benefits of Shrimp Cocktail: *its Waistline Friendly- Shrimp is remarkably low in calories - with four large shrimp having only twenty-two total. Plus, the protein content of shrimp (almost eighteen grams in four of them) is great for building lean body mass when combined with an exercise program. Foods that are high in protein such as shrimp are also more satisfying - so there's less risk of overeating. Shrimp is clean eating at its best.*

Nutritional Information
- Calories: 107.9
- Fat: 0.9 grams
- Carbohydrates: 4 grams
- Protein: 17.8 grams
- Fiber: 0.5 grams

Healthy Nachos

This is a favorite during football season!
Bring this delicious treat to a tailgate party and share with friends!

Ingredients

1.5 pounds of Ground Turkey
2 cans of petite diced tomatoes (low sodium and organic optional)
1 can of cream corn (organic optional)
1 can of black beans (rinsed and organic)
optional 1 jar of salsa (medium)
2 cups of mozzarella cheese
1 tbsp of sea salt
1 tbsp of black ground pepper
1 bag of blue corn gluten free chips- divided

Directions

Preheat oven 350 degrees.
Cook turkey until brown adding in your salt and pepper.
Spray a large backing dish 11x13 with cooking spray.
Using half the bag of chips spread on the bottom.
Spread out the cooked brown turkey.
Layer the cream corn, tomatoes, and black beans on top.
Top with Salsa and then add your cheese.
Bake in oven for 20 min.
Serve with remaining chips.

Nutritional Information
- Calories: 189.5
- Fat: 8.8 grams
- Carbohydrates: 15.6 grams
- Protein: 12.6 grams
- Fiber: 3.5 grams

Cindy's Homemade Guacamole

This is a favorite during football season!
Bring this delicious treat to a tailgate party and share with friends!

Ingredients

2 ripe avocados
1 Lime or Lemon- squeezed
1/2 teaspoon sea salt
¼ teaspoon of freshly grated black pepper
2 tsp of minced garlic
¼ tsp of red pepper flakes
Optional- ¼ cup of Feta Cheese

Directions

Cut avocados in half and remove seed. Scoop out avocado from the peel, put in a mixing bowl. Using a fork, roughly mash the avocado. (Don't overdo it! The guacamole should be a little chunky.) Add the lime or lemon, garlic, salt and pepper and mash some more. Add in the red pepper flakes and feta cheese.

My Guacamole is awesome and I pair it with gluten free chips and carrots. Why is it better to make your own instead of the pre-packaged kind? You know what's going into it and you can control the amount. When you taste it, you know you are getting the health benefits of the Avocados, instead of tons of sodium. Also you can add in different spices to change up the taste.
Benefits of eating Avocados - One of the added benefits of eating avocados, they help reduce levels of cortisol & inflammation, which helps cut down on fat storage in the mid region. Benefits of Feta Cheese-When you choose feta cheese over standard cheddar cheese, you get the cheesy taste with a third less calories.
Feta cheese is also a third lower in fat.

Nutritional Information
- Calories: 162.7
- Fat: 14.7 grams
- Carbohydrates: 8.9 grams
- Protein: 2 grams
- Fiber: 6.3 grams

Spiced Roasted Chickpeas

We are looking for Healthy Side dishes throughout the holidays! This dish is packed with Fiber, Low in Fat, and Low in Carbs

Ingredients

2 15 ounce cans of organic chickpeas- Rinsed and drained
2 tablespoons extra virgin olive oil
1 teaspoon of ground cumin
1 teaspoon of coriander
1 teaspoon of chili powder
Sea salt and ground black peppere

Directions

Preheat the oven to 400 degrees.
In a medium bowl toss the chickpeas with the olive oil, cumin, coriander, chile powder, salt, and pepper.
Spread the chick peas on a cookie sheet.
Roast for 30 min. or until slightly golden.

Nutritional Information
- Calories: 154.7
- Fat: 3.5 grams
- Carbohydrates: 24.5 grams
- Protein: 8.3 grams
- Fiber: 8.4 grams

TRACKING YOUR FOOD, MEAL PLANS, READING FOOD LABEL

TRACKING YOUR FOOD

- You hear all the time that to lose weight, you should track what you eat. Well, a 2008 study published in the American Journal of Preventive Medicine shows that keeping a "food diary" may double your weight loss efforts.
- Researchers kept tabs on 1,685 overweight and obese adults (men and women), whose average weight was 212 pounds. The researchers encouraged participants to adhere to a reduced-calorie, eating plan and asked them record their daily food intake and exercise minutes.
- After 20 weeks, the average weight loss was 13 pounds per person. But researchers discovered something else; the more participants recorded what they ate, the more weight they lost in the end. Participants who did not keep a food diary lost about 9 pounds over the course of the study, while those who recorded their food intake six or more days per week lost 18 pounds - twice as much as those who didn't track any food!

MEAL PLANS

- Meal planning is the advanced planning of the menu for the next few days, or even the entire month. Complete meal planning involves planning the meals to be prepared, as well as the items needed to be purchased to prepare them.

- By filling your plate with foods loaded with nutrients but low in calories, you'll get all the fiber, essential fatty acids, vitamins and minerals you need. You may also find yourself feeling satisfied on fewer calories.

Breakfast (300 calories)	Lunch (450 calories)	Mid-afternoon Snack (200 calories)	Dinner (500 calories)
¾ cup 100% fruit juice 1 slice whole-grain toast 1 oz whole-grain breakfast cereal ½ cup fat-free milk	2 oz meat, poultry, or fish 2 slices whole-grain bread 2 pieces lettuce 2 slices tomato ½ cup baby carrots ½ cup berries or 1 piece of fruit 1 cup fat-free milk	5 whole-grain crackers 1 tbsp peanut or other nut butter ½ fat-free milk	1 cup vegetable soup 2 oz meat, poultry, or fish 1 medium sweet potato or white potato ½ cup broccoli 1 cup fat-free milk

Nutrition Facts
Serving Size 3 oz (85g)
Servings Per Container 1

Amount Per Serving	
Calories 180	Calories from Fat 90

	% Daily Value*
Total Fat 10g	15%
Saturated Fat 40g	20%
Trans Fat 0.5g	
Cholesterol 70mg	23%
Sodium 60mg	3%
Total Carbohydrate 0g	0%
Dietary Fiber 0g	0%
Sugars 0g	
Protein 22g	

| Vitamin A 0% | • | Vitamin C 0% |
| Calcium 2% | • | Iron 15% |

*Percent Daily Values are based on a 2,000 calorie diet. Your daily values may be higher or lower depending on your caloric needs:

	Calories:	2,000	2,500
Total Fat	Less than	65g	80g
Saturated Fat	Less than	20g	25g
Cholesterol	Less than	300mg	300mg
Sodiuum	Less than	2,400mg	2,400mg
Total Carbohydrate		300g	375g
Dietary Fiber		25g	30g

Calories per gram:
Fat 9 • Carbohydrate 4 • Protein 4

READING FOOD LABEL

- The Nutrition Facts label is a boxed panel required by the Food and Drug Administration on most packaged food and beverage products. The Nutrition Facts label provides detailed information about the nutrient content of the product. The label is intended to help you make healthier choices. The required information is standard, but the specific nutrients vary depending on the food product.

- You can read the Nutrition Facts label to determine the amounts of such nutrients as fat, sodium and fiber in specific products. Knowing this information can help you decide whether a food or beverage fits in to your eating plan or is appropriate if you have certain health conditions, such as high blood pressure or high cholesterol. It also enables you to compare similar products to see which one might be a healthier choice.

The numbers on produce – what does it mean?

Although they seem like a nuisance, the stickers or labels attached to fruit and some vegetables have more of a function than helping scan the price at the checkout stand. The PLU code, or price lookup number printed on the sticker, also tells you how the fruit was grown. By reading the PLU code, you can tell if the fruit was genetically modified, organically grown or produced with chemical fertilizers, fungicides, or herbicides. Here are the basics of what you should know:

• If there are only four numbers in the PLU, this means that the produce was grown conventionally or "traditionally" with the use of pesticides. The last four letters of the PLU code are simply what kind of vegetable or fruit. An example is that all bananas are labeled with the code of 4011.

• If there are five numbers in the PLU code, and the number starts with "8", this tells you that the item is a genetically modified fruit or vegetable. Genetically modified fruits and vegetables trump being organic. So, it is impossible to eat organic produce that are grown from genetically modified seeds. A genetically engineered (GE or GMO) banana would be: 84011

• If there are five numbers in the PLU code, and the number starts with "9", this tells you that the produce was grown organically and is not genetically modified. An organic banana would be: 94011

Incidentally, the adhesive used to attach the stickers is considered food-grade, but the stickers themselves aren't edible.

LUNCH

"Its no longer about skinny, now it's about healthy!"

"Fit is not a destination, its a way of LIFE."

Stuffed Peppers ⓖⓕ

This is a family friendly recipe with just the right combination of high protein and complex carbohydrates.

Ingredients

4 bell peppers, halved and seeded
¼ cup of water
2 cups of yellow rice cooked
2 cups of shredded cheddar cheese
1lb of ground turkey, browned and drained

Directions

Arrange peppers in a 9x13 glass baking dish, cut-side down. Pour ¼ cup water in bottom of dish. Cover dish tightly with foil and bake in preheated oven at 425 for 20 minutes. Do not turn oven off! Drain peppers on paper towels and place peppers back in dish, cut-side up. Stir in 1 ½ cup of cheese and ground turkey into prepared rice. Fill the peppers with rice mix and sprinkle remaining cheese on tops of peppers. Bake uncovered for 5 minutes, or until cheese is melted.

Nutritional Information
- Calories: 229.7
- Fat: 6.7 grams
- Carbohydrates: 22.8 grams
- Protein: 19.9 grams
- Fiber: 2.4 grams

Creamed Corn Mint Couscous

This dish is great paired with Cindy's Sautéed Mint Salmon

Ingredients

1 box of couscous
2 cups of low sodium chicken broth/ or water
1 cup of cream of corn
1 tsp of sea salt
1 tsp of fresh ground pepper
Optional 1/3 cup of grated Parmesan cheese

Directions

In a medium pan boil the 2 cups of chicken broth/ or water.
Pour in the couscous and remove from heat and cover.
Let sit for 5 min. and then use a fork to mix. Stir in the cream of corn, salt, and pepper.
Optional to add 1/3 cup of Parmesan cheese.

Nutritional Information
- Calories: 273.1
- Fat: 6 grams
- Carbohydrates: 49.5 grams
- Protein: 8.4 grams
- Fiber: 4.7 grams

Papaya Salad - Thai Cooking GF DF V

Over the holidays I had the most amazing experience, I got to travel to Thailand. The culture was awesome, but even better was the food. Thai food is not only packed with a lot of flavor, but most dishes are healthy for you too!

Ingredients

1 medium dark green papaya
3 garlic cloves (kratiem)
1 red Thai Chilies (prikkheenoo)
1 tomato, cut into wedges
½ cup of chopped green beans
1 tablespoon of fish sauce
¼ cup of lime juice (1 lime squeezed) (ma-kaampiag)
1 cup of unsalted peanuts

Directions

Peel the papaya and rinse with running water to remove the acid. Remove the seeds and shred the papaya with a grater. Set aside in a bowl of ice water for crispiness. Place the garlic cloves and the chilies in a mortar and mash with a pestle until crushed into chunks. Place the papaya and the remaining ingredients in the mortar and gently combine all ingredients by mixing with the pestle and a spoon. Serve cold and enjoy!

Nutritional Information
- Calories: 245.8
- Fat: 5.4 grams
- Carbohydrates: 49.4 grams
- Protein: 6.7 grams
- Fiber: 8.7 grams

Sloppy Joe's

*This is a healthy meal and the kids are going to love it!
Lots of flavor and low on calories!*

Ingredients

2 ½ pounds of ground turkey
½ cup chopped onion
½ cup chopped green bell pepper
½ cup chopped tomato
1 cup no-salt added ketchup
7 tablespoon barbecue sauce
2 tablespoons yellow mustard
1 tablespoon vinegar
½ teaspoon celery seed
½ teaspoon ground black pepper
½ teaspoon red pepper flakes
8 hamburger buns

Directions

Heat a nonstick skillet over medium heat; cook and stir turkey, onion, bell pepper, and tomato until turkey is crumbly and longer pink, about 5 min. Stir in ketchup, barbeque sauce, mustard, vinegar, celery seed, black pepper, and red pepper flakes. Reduce heat to low and simmer for 10 min., stirring occasionally.
Serve and enjoy!

Nutritional Information
- Calories: 219.5
- Fat: 7 grams
- Carbohydrates: 29.8 grams
- Protein: 22.4 grams
- Fiber: 0.5 grams

Sundried Tomato Grilled Chicken Flatbread Pizza

This is a healthy option with a lot of pizazz to America's favorite food.
You can use flat bread, tortilla shells or make your own dough.
I usually find the flatouts in the bakery section of the grocery store and they come
in a variety of flavors and are made of whole grains.
In this recipe we do not use tomato sauce.
This is a fast and easy recipe to make that is low in calories
and fat and the whole family will love it!

Ingredients

2 Large Boneless Chicken Breasts- precook (this recipe is great for making when having left over chicken breasts)
3 Flatbreads
1 jar of sliced sundried tomatoes in oil
1 tbsp of oregano
1 tbsp of basil
2 cups of shredded mozzarella cheese; divided
1 tsp of sea salt
1 tsp of ground black pepper

Directions

Preheat oven 350. Bake the flatbreads alone for 3-5 min. Coat the flatbreads with olive oil. Cut the grilled chicken breasts into bite size pieces. In a large bowl, combine chicken, entire jar of sundried tomatoes, and 1 cup of cheese. Add in dry ingredients. Spoon grilled chicken mixture onto flat breads. Top with remaining cup of cheese and bake for 5-7 min. or until cheese is melted.

Nutritional Information
- Calories: 292.6
- Fat: 31.4 grams
- Carbohydrates: 24.5 grams
- Protein: 33.8 grams
- Fiber: 11.7 grams

Jerk Turkey Sloppy Joe's

Ingredients

2 tablespoons vegetable oil
1.5 pounds lean ground turkey or turkey breast
1 onion, chopped
1 Palermo pepper, seeded and finely chopped
1 red bell pepper, seeded and chopped
3 to 4 cloves garlic, chopped

Sauce

2 tablespoons cider vinegar
2 tablespoons dark brown sugar
1 tablespoon Worcestershire sauce

Kosher salt and freshly ground black pepper
1 tablespoon paprika or smoked sweet paprika
1-inch piece fresh ginger, grated or minced
1 teaspoon allspice
1/2 teaspoon ground cinnamon
Freshly grated nutmeg
2 tablespoons chopped fresh thyme leaves
Small handful cilantro leaves, finely chopped or 1/2 a palmful ground coriander

1 lime, juiced
1 cup tomato sauce
4 rolls heated over grill pan
Chopped scallions, for garnish
Chopped cilantro leaves, for garnish

Directions

Heat the oil in a large skillet over medium-high heat. When the oil ripples and is hot, add the meat and brown. Add the onions, chile, bell pepper, garlic and salt and pepper, to taste. Stir in the paprika, ginger, allspice, cinnamon, nutmeg, thyme and cilantro. Stir occasionally for 8 to 10 min. In a small bowl combine the vinegar, sugar, Worcestershire sauce, lime juice, and tomato sauce. Stir the sauce into the turkey mixture. Simmer for a few minutes, then serve on rolls with a garnish of scallions, chopped pickles, and chopped cilantro.

Nutritional Information
- Calories: 155.5
- Fat: 3.85 grams
- Carbohydrates: 4.5 grams
- Protein: 28.2 grams
- Fiber: 1.2 grams

Cauliflower Au Gratin

*Did you know Cauliflower is a cancer fighting food?
Cauliflower contains sulforaphane, a sulfur compound that has also been shown to kill cancer stem cells, thereby slowing tumor growth. Some researchers believe eliminating cancer stem cells may be key to controlling cancer.*

Ingredients

1 (3-pound) head cauliflower, cut into large florets
Kosher salt
4 tablespoons (1/2 stick) smart balance butter spread, divided
3 tablespoons almond flour
2 cups hot skim milk
1/2 teaspoon freshly ground black pepper
1/4 teaspoon grated nutmeg
3/4 cup freshly grated Gruyere, divided
1/2 cup freshly grated Parmesan
1/4 cup ground up rolled oats (or Bread Crumbs)

Directions

Preheat the oven to 375 degrees F. Cook the cauliflower florets in a large pot of boiling salted water for 5 to 6 minutes, until tender but still firm. Drain. Meanwhile, melt 2 tablespoons of the butter in a medium saucepan over low heat. Add the flour, stirring constantly with a wooden spoon for 2 min. Pour the hot milk into the butter-flour mixture and stir until it comes to a boil. Boil, whisking constantly, for 1 minute, or until thickened. Off the heat, add 1 teaspoon of salt, the pepper, nutmeg, 1/2 cup of the Gruyere, and the Parmesan. Pour 1/3 of the sauce on the bottom of an 8 by 11 by 2-inch baking dish. Place the drained cauliflower on top and then spread the rest of the sauce evenly on top. Combine the ground up rolled oats with the remaining 1/4 cup of Gruyere and sprinkle on top. Melt the remaining 2 tablespoons of butter and drizzle over the gratin. Sprinkle with salt and pepper. Bake for 30 min., until the top is browned.

Nutritional Information
- Calories: 122.8
- Fat: 7.6 grams
- Carbohydrates: 7.3 grams
- Protein: 9.7 grams
- Fiber: 2.7 grams

Jerk Turkey Burgers with Apples

*After many visits to Jamaica, I always love Jerk seasoning.
I love to put in my burgers and on chicken!*

Ingredients

1 pound ground turkey
1 tablespoon jerk seasoning, plus more for sprinkling
1 small green apple, peeled and grated
1/2 cup finely chopped scallions
1/4 cup panko breadcrumbs
Kosher salt and freshly ground pepper
1/4 cup olive oil mayonnaise by Kraft, plus more for brushing
1/4 cup pineapple chutney
3 cups shredded purple cabbage
1 carrot, shredded
Canola oil, for the grill
4 hamburger buns or challah rolls, split

Directions

Preheat a grill or grill pan to medium high. Mix the turkey, jerk seasoning, apple, 1/4 cup scallions and the panko in a bowl; season with salt and pepper. Form into four 1-inch-thick patties and make a small indentation in the middle of each with your thumb to prevent it from puffing up on the grill. Refrigerate.

Whisk the mayonnaise and chutney in a large bowl. Add the cabbage, carrot and the remaining 1/4 cup scallions, season with salt and pepper and toss to coat. Brush the grill with canola oil. Grill the turkey patties until browned and cooked through, 4 to 5 min. Brush the cut sides of the buns with mayonnaise and sprinkle with jerk seasoning; toast on the grill, about 30 seconds.

Serve the burgers and slaw on the buns.

Nutritional Information
- Calories: 182.6
- Fat: 8.2 grams
- Carbohydrates: 5.1 grams
- Protein: 22.8 grams
- Fiber: 1.1 grams

Cindy's Healthy Chicken Tacos (GF)

*Who doesn't love a good taco?
Well no guilt here and they are packed full of flavor with some great spices!*

Ingredients

1 teaspoon pure chile powder
1 teaspoon sea salt
1/2 teaspoon ground cumin
1/2 teaspoon onion powder
1/4 teaspoon garlic powder
1 tablespoon cornstarch
1/4 cup water
3 tablespoons extra-virgin olive oil

1 pound chicken tenderloins (organic) cut into 1/2-inch pieces
1 green bell pepper - cored, seeded and cut into thin strips
1 medium onion, thinly sliced
2 tablespoons fresh lime juice, plus lime wedges for serving
8 pack of whole grain black bean shells
Dark green spring mix (lettuce)
1/2 cup diced tomatoes, 1 avocado
1 cup Mozzarella cheese

Directions

In a resealable plastic bag, combine the chile powder with the salt, cumin, onion powder, garlic powder, cornstarch, water and 2 tablespoons of the oil. Add the chicken, bell pepper and onion, seal and knead gently to coat. Refrigerate for 30 min. Heat the remaining 1 tablespoon of oil in a large nonstick skillet until shimmering. Empty the contents of the bag into the skillet and cook over high heat, stirring occasionally, until the vegetables are crisp-tender and the chicken is cooked through, about 6 min. Remove from the heat and stir in the lime juice. Transfer the chicken and vegetables to a large bowl and serve with the warmed tortillas, diced tomatoes, lettuce, cheese, salsa, guacamole, and lime wedges. In addition add whole grain chips for a side.

Nutritional Information
- *Calories: 183*
- *Fat: 5.9 grams*
- *Carbohydrates: 10.8 grams*
- *Protein: 21.5 grams*
- *Fiber: 1.6 grams*

Cindy's Guacamole

Ingredients: 1 cloveof garlic, 1/8 tsp sea salt, 1/2 of lime-fresh squeezed, 1 avocado. **Directions:** Mix together in bowl with fork, chunky is better.

Nutritional Information
- *Calories: 76.4*
- *Fat: 6.7 grams*
- *Carbohydrates: 4.7 grams*
- *Protein: 1 grams*
- *Fiber: 3.1 grams*

Roasted Parmesan Cauliflower

Love this recipe! Super simple with lots of flavor!

Ingredients

1 small to medium head cauliflower, cut into florets, about 6 cups cauliflower florets
2 teaspoons crushed garlic
4 tablespoons olive oil
1 teaspoon salt
1/2 teaspoon freshly ground black pepper
1/2 cup fresh grated Parmesan cheese

Directions

Line a large baking pan with foil; spray lightly with cooking spray. Heat oven to 425°.
In a large bowl or food storage bag toss the cauliflower florets with the olive oil, garlic, seasonings, and Parmesan cheese.
Spread the cauliflower out on the prepared baking pan.
Roast for 25 to 30 min., turning every 10 min., or until tender and lightly browned.

Nutritional Information
- Calories: 156.8
- Fat: 11.1 grams
- Carbohydrates: 8.8 grams
- Protein: 8.2 grams
- Fiber: 3.7 grams

Grilled Chicken over a Wheat Spaghetti Alfredo topped with Bell Peppers & Tomatoes

Here is another fantastic recipe to satisfy your taste for Alfredo Sauce without all the Fat!

Ingredients

4 Thin Sliced Chicken Breasts
1 tablespoon of Cumin
1 tablespoon of Chili Powder
2 Cloves of Garlic
1 tablespoon of onion powder
1 tablespoon of garlic powder
1/2 tablespoon of black pepper
1/2 tablespoon of sea salt
1 tablespoon of Italian Seasoning
3 tablespoon of smart balance butter spread (Seperated)
1 bell pepper
2 Roma Tomatoes
1 package of Whole grain Spaghetti noodles
1/2 cup of fat free cream cheese
1/2 tablespoon of corn starch or wheat germ
1/2 cup of skim milk

Directions

In a skillet, melt 1 tablespoon butter spread. Grill chicken and peppers in a skillet until no longer pink. Sprinkle Cumin, Italian Seasoning & Chili Powder on chicken.
Boil your pasta as directed on box. In a medium sauce pan over low-medium heat, melt 2 tablespoons of smart balance butter and add garlic. Add in skim milk, corn starch, and fat free cream cheese - turn down to simmer-low. Add in salt, pepper, garlic powder, and onion powder. Stir often until even consistency and do not let sauce boil. Place your noodles on the plate, top with Alfredo sauce, side of chicken and top with cooked peppers and fresh sliced Roma tomatoes.

Nutritional Information
- Calories: 253.8
- Fat: 7.1 grams
- Carbohydrates: 33.9 grams
- Protein: 16.2 grams
- Fiber: 4.9 grams

Anaheim Sword Fish Tacos

This recipe is full of flavor, easy to make, and inexpensive!

Ingredients

1 teaspoon of oilive oil
1 anaheim chile pepper, chopped
1 leek, chopped
2 cloves garlic, crushed
sea salt & pepper to taste
1 cup of low sodium chicken broth
2 large tomatoes, diced
1/2 teaspoon of cumin
1 1/2 pounds of sword fish filets
1 lime
12 Corn Tortillas

Directions

Heat the oil in a large skillet over medium heat, and saute the chile, leek, and garlic until tender and lightly browned. Season with salt and pepper to taste.
Mix the chicken broth and tomatoes into the skillet, and season with cumin. Bring to a boil. Reduce heat to low. Place the swordfish into the mixture. Sprinkle with lime juice.
Cook 15-20 minutes until the swordfish is easily flaked with a fork.
Wrap in warm tortilla shells and serve!

Nutritional Information
- Calories: 365.1
- Fat: 12.5 grams
- Carbohydrates: 34 grams
- Protein: 32.2 grams
- Fiber: 8.2 grams

Raw Zucchini with Creamy Tomato Sauce GF DF V

This Raw recipe is amazing! You will think you are eating pasta!
The creamy sauce is delicious and is dairy free.
I paired this with fresh caught Cobia

Ingredients

4 medium zucchini
20 cherry tomatoes
2 cloves of garlic
2 tablespoons of tahini
3 teaspoons of dried basil
1 teaspoon oregano
1 teaspoon sea salt
1 teaspoon ground black pepper

Directions

Process zucchini into spirals or matchsticks and set aside.
Add all ingredients into a food processor, blend until smooth.
Top zucchini with sauce and serve. Enjoy!

Nutritional Information
- Calories: 76.2
- Fat: 5 grams
- Carbohydrates: 9.3 grams
- Protein: 1.2 grams
- Fiber: 1.4 grams

Chicken Shawarma

One of Jason's favorite dishes, we LOVE Greek food!

Ingredients

1 Zucchini
1/2 cup of fresh cilantro, chopped
1/4 cup of red onion
Zest from 1 lime and juice from 2 limes
1/2 teaspoon of honey
1 small avocado, diced
sea salt & pepper to taste

Ingredients for Sauce

1/2 cupplain 2% reduced-fat Greek yogurt
2 tablespoons tahini
2 teaspoons fresh lemon juice
1/4 teaspoon salt
1 garlic clove, minced

Remaining ingredients

Cooking spray
4 (6-inch) pitas
1 cup chopped romaine lettuce
8 (1/4-inch-thick) tomato slices

Directions

Preheat grill to medium-high heat. To prepare chicken, combine first 6 ingredients in a medium bowl. Add chicken to bowl; toss well to coat. Let stand at room temperature 20 min. To prepare sauce, combine yogurt and next 4 ingredients (through 1 garlic clove), stirring with a whisk. Thread 2 chicken strips onto each of 8 (12-inch) skewers. Place kebabs on a grill rack coated with cooking spray; grill 4 min. on each side or until done. Place pitas on grill rack; grill 1 minute on each side or until lightly toasted. Place 1 pita on each of 4 plates; top each serving with 1/4 cup lettuce and 2 tomato slices. Top each serving with 4 chicken pieces; drizzle each serving with 2 tablespoons sauce.

Nutritional Information
- Calories: 349.2
- Fat: 9.5 grams
- Carbohydrates: 36 grams
- Protein: 32.1 grams
- Fiber: 8.2 grams

Gluten Free Lemon Pasta with Oven Roasted Shrimp ⓖⓕ

This was a hit for my non gluten free friends, they couldn't tell a difference and they loved every bite!

Ingredients

2 pounds (17 to 21 count) shrimp, peeled and deveined
Good Extra Virgin olive oil
Sea salt and freshly ground black pepper
1 pound Gluten Free Angel Hair Pasta
4 tablespoons (1/2 stick) smart balance butter spread
2 lemons, zested and juiced

Directions

Preheat the oven to 400 degrees F.
Place the shrimp on a sheet pan with 1 tablespoon olive oil, 1/2 teaspoon salt, and 1/2 teaspoon pepper. Toss well, spread them in 1 layer, and roast for 6 to 8 minutes, just until they're pink and cooked through. Meanwhile, drizzle some olive oil in a large pot of boiling salted water, add the angel hair, and cook about 3 min. Drain the pasta, reserving some of the cooking liquid. Quickly toss the angel hair with the melted butter spread, 1/4 cup olive oil, the lemon zest, lemon juice, 2 teaspoons sea salt, 1 teaspoon pepper and about 1/2 cup of the reserved cooking liquid. Add the shrimp and serve hot.

Nutritional Information
- Calories: 266.2
- Fat: 9 grams
- Carbohydrates: 30 grams
- Protein: 29.8 grams
- Fiber: 4.4 grams

Lemon Pepper Chicken

Ingredients

2 tsp of butter with olive oil
1 lb of thinly sliced organic chicken breasts tenderloins - cut into strips
1 tbsp of black pepper
1/2 fresh squeezed lemon

Directions

Melt butter in a small skillet.
Pepper the skillet with 1/2 tablespoon of the pepper, then lay the chicken breast onto the pepper. Squeeze fresh lemon juice onto the chicken, then season with the remaining pepper. Saute chicken breast for about 5 to 7 min., then turn to the other side, squeeze lemon juice onto the other side and saute for another 5 to 7 min. (or until chicken is cooked through and juices run clear).

Nutritional Information
- Calories: 185
- Fat: 6.5 grams
- Carbohydrates: 9.5 grams
- Protein: 21.8 grams
- Fiber: 0.9 grams

Healthy Chicken Flat Bread Pizza

This is a great recipe if you are short on time and the kids want pizza.
No guilt here, just sit down and enjoy.

Ingredients

4 whole grain flat bread (you can use thin pita bread)
1 1/2 cups of sliced grilled chicken
1/2 cup sun-dried tomato packed in oil, coarsely chopped
6 leaves fresh basil, coarsely chopped
3 cups grated mozzarella cheese
1 teaspoon sea salt
1 teaspoon ground black pepper
1 teaspoon red pepper flakes

Directions

Per heat oven to 375. Mix all the ingredients together (except the bread) in a bowl. Use your hands. It's easier.
Lay the flat breads on a baking sheet - spray with cooking spray- Mound the mixture on the flat bread, spreading to the edges. Place in oven- Bake for 3-5 min. or until cheese is melted- When it is melted, it's done. (If you leave it in too long, the bread will burn).
Put it on a bread board and cut it with a pizza cutter.

Nutritional Information
- Calories: 252
- Fat: 9 grams
- Carbohydrates: 28 grams
- Protein: 13.5 grams
- Fiber: 1.4 grams

Spicing Up Your Meals When Eating Clean

Healthy food has an undeserved reputation for being boring or bland. Whole, fresh foods are actually delicious on their own, with no added seasoning. Unfortunately, many of us have been jaded by too much sodium, sugar, and additives in our food. But there are healthy ways to add flavor to clean foods. Here are some herbs and spices you can use in your daily cooking:

- **Basil:** This bright-green delicate leaf contains flavonoids that act as powerful antioxidants. It's also high in vitamins A and K and has a good amount of potassium and manganese. You can grow basil plants on a sunny windowsill throughout the year or grow it in your garden and preserve it by freezing or drying it. Use peppery and minty basil in tomato sauces, salad dressings, pesto, sandwich spreads, soups, and chicken, beef, pork, and fish dishes.

- **Marjoram:** This fragrant herb contains many phytochemicals — including terpenes, which are anti-inflammatory — lutein, and beta carotene. Plus, it has lots of vitamin C and vitamin D. Marjoram is delicious in any dish made using beef and is perfect with vegetables like tomatoes, peas, carrots, and spinach. Together with bay leaf, parsley, thyme, and tarragon, it makes a bouquet garni to use in stews and soups.

- **Mint:** Mothers used to offer mint to kids for upset stomachs because it soothes an irritated GI tract. But did you know it may be a weapon against cancer, too? It contains a phytochemical called perillyl alcohol, which can stop the formation of some cancer cells. Mint is a good source of beta carotene, folate, and
riboflavin. Use it in teas, in desserts, as part of a fruit salad or lettuce salad, or as a garnish for puddings.

- **Oregano:** Used in Italian dishes, this strong herb is a potent antioxidant with the phytochemicals lutein and beta carotene. It's a good source of iron, fiber, calcium, vitamin C, vitamin A, and omega-3 fatty acids. Who knew that spaghetti sauce could be so good for you? Add spicy and pepper oregano to salad dressings, soups, sauces, gravies, meat dishes, and pork recipes.

- **Parsley:** Do you ever wonder what's happened to all the parsley garnish that has been left on plates in restaurants over the years? If only people knew then how healthy it really is! This mild and leafy herb is an excellent source of vitamin C, iron, calcium, and potassium. Plus, it's packed with flavonoids, which are strong antioxidants, and folate, which can help reduce the risk of heart disease. Use it in everything from salads as a leafy green to rice pilafs, grilled fish, and sauces and gravies.

- **Rosemary:** Rosemary contains terpenes, which slow down free radical development and stop inflammation. Terpenes may also block some estrogens, which cause breast cancer. Use this pungent and piney herb in soups, stews, meat, and chicken dishes. Chop some fresh rosemary to roast a chicken, cook with lamb or beef, or mix with olive oil for a dip for warm whole-wheat bread.

- **Sage:** Sage contains the flavonoid phytochemicals apigenin and luteolin and some phenolic acids that act as anti-inflammatory agents and antioxidants. Perhaps sage's most impressive effect may be against Alzheimer's disease by inhibiting the increase in AChE inhibitors. Its dusky, earthy aroma and flavor are delicious in classic turkey stuffing (as well as the turkey itself), spaghetti sauces, soups and stews, and frittatas and omelets.

- **Tarragon:** This herb tastes like licorice with a slightly sweet flavor and is delicious with chicken or fish. It's a great source of phytosterols and can reduce the stickiness of platelets in your blood. Tarragon is rich in beta carotene and potassium, too. Use it as a salad green or as part of a salad dressing or mix it with Greek yogurt to use as an appetizer dip.

- **Thyme:** This herb is a good source of vitamin K, manganese, and the monoterpene thymol, which has antibacterial properties and may help protect against tumor development. It's fresh, slightly minty, and lemony tasting, making it a great addition to everything from egg dishes to pear desserts to recipes featuring chicken and fish.

- **Cinnamon:** The aroma of cinnamon is one of the most enticing in cooking; just the smell can help improve brain function! It can also reduce blood sugar levels, LDL cholesterol, triglycerides, and overall cholesterol levels. Cinnamaldehyde, an organic compound in cinnamon (go figure!), prevents clumping of blood platelets, and other compounds in this spice are anti-inflammatory. Add cinnamon to coffee and tea, use it in desserts and curries, and sprinkle some on oatmeal for a great breakfast.

- **Cloves:** These flower buds are a great source of manganese and omega-3 fatty acids. They contain eugenol, which helps reduce toxicity from pollutants and prevent joint inflammation, and the flavonoids kaempferol and rhamnetin, which act as antioxidants. Cloves are a great addition to hot tea and coffee as well as many dessert recipes, including fruit compote and apple desserts.

- **Cumin:** This spice is rich in antioxidants, which may help reduce the risk of cancer. It also has iron and manganese, which help keep your immune system strong and healthy. Add cumin to Middle Eastern recipes, rice pilafs, stir-fried vegetables, and Tex-Mex dishes.

- **Nutmeg:** Nutmeg is rich in calcium, potassium, magnesium, phosphorus, and vitamins A and C. It can help reduce blood pressure, acts as an antioxidant, and has antifungal properties. The lacy covering on nutmeg is used to make mace. Keep a whole nutmeg in a tiny jar along with a mini rasp to grate it fresh into dishes with spinach, add it to hot tea, use it in curry powder, and add it to rice pudding and other desserts.

- **Turmeric:** This spice is one of the healthiest foods on the planet. Curcumin, a phytochemical in turmeric, can stop cancer cells from reproducing and spreading, slow Alzheimer's disease progression, and help control weight. In fact, researchers are currently studying curcumin as a cancer fighter, painkiller, and antiseptic. Turmeric gives foods a pretty yellow color and is an inexpensive
substitute for saffron. Use it in Indian foods, egg salads, sauces, tea, and fish and chicken recipes.

DINNER

"Strive for progress, not perfection."

"Your body is a reflection of your lifestyle."

Cindy's Low Fat Chicken & Vegetable Fettuccine Alfredo

This is a great alternative to your favorite Alfredo without the FAT!

Ingredients

1 cup 1% low-fat milk (skim may be used, but creates a thinner sauce)
1 1/2 tablespoons butter (made with olive oil)
1 1/2 tablespoons whole wheat flour
3 tablespoons parmesan cheese
1/2 teaspoon minced garlic
1/2 tsp of pepper
1 tsp of sea salt
Whole grain Fettuccine noodles
2 boneless chicken breasts (cut into strips)
3 tablespoons of olive oil
1 bell pepper- cut into slices
1/2 cup of thin sliced mushrooms
1 squash- cut into thin slices
1 tsp of basil

Directions

Alfredo Sauce
The key here is patience, add all ingredients gradually! Melt butter in sauce pan on stove top with medium heat. Gradually whisk in flour. This will create a yellow paste. Gradually add milk, whisking until incorporated and no lumps are present. Continue to whisk until hot. Usually 3-5 minutes. The longer you cook the base (without the cheese) the thicker the sauce will be. Add parmesan slowly, again whisking until incorporated. Add crushed garlic and pepper. Cook for 2 minutes or until cheese is melted. Remove from heat. Cook Whole Grain Fettuccine as directed, rinse and set to side.

Chicken
In a skillet- heat 3 tablespoons of olive oil over medium heat. Add in chicken and parsley. Sauté chicken until lightly browned after 5 min., toss in squash, bell pepper, and mushrooms. Sauté until vegetables become soft

Nutritional Information
- *Calories: 206*
- *Fat: 8.1 grams*
- *Carbohydrates: 16.3 grams*
- *Protein: 16.5 grams*
- *Fiber: 0.8 grams*

Ground Turkey & Couscous

*This is a fast and easy recipe, especially if you have left overs.
I usually throw everything but the kitchen sink into left over couscous.*

Ingredients

1lb Ground Turkey
1 cup of dried (Cooked and Rinsed) Black Beans or
1 can of black beans (drained and rinsed to reduce sodium)
1 can of diced tomatoes (drained)
3/4 cup of sliced mushrooms
1 medium yellow onion- finely chopped
1/2 tsp of paprika
1 tsp of hot sauce
1/2 tsp of chipolte powder
1/2 tsp of chile powder
1 tsp of black pepper
1 tsp of sea salt
1 tbsp of olive oil
1 box of whole wheat couscous

Directions

Place olive oil in a large cooking skillet.
On medium heat brown turkey and cook until onion is soft. Add in all spices.
Once turkey is brown add in mushrooms, tomatoes, and black beans.

Reduce heat and simmer for 30 min, stirring occasionally. Serve over couscous and add in a leafy salad for your daily intake of greens.

Nutritional Information
- Calories: 151
- Fat: 6.3 grams
- Carbohydrates: 13.4 grams
- Protein: 11.5 grams
- Fiber: 2.4 grams

Amazing Fish Tacos

This is a staple in our house, I must fix fish tacos at least once a week!
High protein, low fat, and tasty!

Ingredients

1 lime
1 cup grape tomatoes, chopped
1/2 cup cilantro, chopped
1/2 jalapeno, seeded and finely chopped
1/2 sweet onion, finely chopped
1/2 teaspoon salt
1 cup plain nonfat Greek yogurt

2 tablespoons mayonnaise
2 cups green or red cabbage, sliced into narrow strips
1 tablespoon olive oil
1 pound tilapia fillets
1/4 teaspoon chili powder
1/4 teaspoon black pepper
8 small whole wheat tortillas
1 avocado, cut into 8 long slices

Directions

Cut lime in half. Squeeze juice from half and slice other half into 4 thin wedges. In a bowl, combine tomatoes, cilantro, jalapeno, onion, 1/4 teaspoon salt, and half the lime juice. In another bowl, mix together yogurt, mayonnaise, and remaining lime juice. Combine cabbage and 2 tablespoons of yogurt sauce in another bowl; reserve extra sauce. Heat olive oil in a large pan. Sprinkle tilapia with chili powder, black pepper, and remaining 1/4 teaspoon salt; cook 3 min. Turn; cook 2 min. Place 2 tortillas, 1 lime wedge, and 1/4 of the tilapia on each plate. Serve with salsa, cabbage, avocado, and sauce.

Nutritional Information
- Calories: 466.7
- Fat: 20 grams
- Carbohydrates: 42.3 grams
- Protein: 35.8 grams
- Fiber: 11.3 grams

Ground Turkey, Black Bean, and Couscous Salad

*As you can tell we love couscous,
its fast and goes with just about every meal.*

Ingredients

1 cup uncooked couscous
1 lb ground turkey
1 1/4 cups low sodium chicken broth
3 tablespoons extra virgin olive oil
2 tablespoons fresh lime juice
1 teaspoon red wine vinegar
1/2 teaspoon ground cumin

8 green onions, chopped
1 med yellow onion, sliced finely
1 green bell pepper, seeded and chopped
1 red bell pepper, seeded and chopped
1/4 cup chopped fresh cilantro
1 cup frozen corn kernels, thawed
2 (15 ounce) cans black beans, drained and rinsed
salt and pepper to taste

Directions

In large skillet with 1 tablespoon of olive oil, sautée green bell pepper and onion. Once soft add in ground turkey and brown - set aside. Bring chicken broth to a boil in a 2 quart or larger sauce pan and stir in the couscous. Cover the pot and remove from heat. Let stand for 5 min. In a large bowl, whisk together the olive oil, lime juice, vinegar and cumin. Add green onions, red pepper, cilantro, corn and beans and toss to coat. Fluff the couscous well, breaking up any chunks. Add to the bowl with the vegetables and mix well. Stir in ground turkey mixture Season with salt and pepper to taste and serve at once or refrigerate until ready to serve.

Nutritional Information
- *Calories: 240*
- *Fat: 6.5 grams*
- *Carbohydrates: 26.5 grams*
- *Protein: 19.2 grams*
- *Fiber: 5 grams*

Cindy's Lemon Parmesan Tilapia GF

If you have a hard time getting the kids to try fish, this is a great recipe! Mild fish and the parmesan gives it a nice flavor and goes well with the fresh squeezed lemon.

Ingredients

4 tilapia fillets
3 tablespoons fresh lemon juice
1 tablespoon smart balance butter, melted
2 cloves garlic, finely chopped
1 teaspoon dried parsley flakes
pepper to taste
1/3 cup of Parmesan

Directions

Preheat oven to 375 degrees F (190 degrees C). Spray a baking dish with non-stick cooking spray. Rinse tilapia fillets under cool water, and pat dry with paper towels. Place fillets in baking dish. Pour lemon juice over fillets, then drizzle butter on top. Sprinkle with garlic, parsley, pepper, and Parmesan. Bake in preheated oven until the fish is white and flakes when pulled apart with a fork, about 30 min.

Nutritional Information
- Calories: 177
- Fat: 10.5 grams
- Carbohydrates: 1.2 grams
- Protein: 19.6 grams
- Fiber: 0 grams

Cindy's Feta Cheese Tilapia GF

Again another great fish dish for the kids to try, a lot of flavor and high in protein!

Ingredients

4 Tilapia Filet's- dry
1 lemon
1 tbsp of olive oil
2 tbsp of smart balance butter - melted
2 oz feta cheese- crumbled
2 cloves of garlic

1 tbsp of olive oil
1/3 cup of fresh parsley
1/2 tsp of black pepper
2 Roma tomatoes diced
1 tbsp of dill weed
1/2 tsp of sea salt

Directions

Preheat oven 350 degrees. In a 9 x 13 glass dish- coat with olive oil. Lay the 4 filet's in dish. Pour lemon juice and butter spread over filet's.
Combine all ingredients except for feta cheese and top each filet.
Bake in oven for 20 minutes. Remove from oven and sprinkle crumbled feta over each filet and bake for an additional 5 min. I made sauteed Brussel sprouts and couscous as a side item with this recipe - YUMMY! And of course added a fresh salad...

Nutritional Information
- *Calories: 211.7*
- *Fat: 11.5 grams*
- *Carbohydrates: 13.9 grams*
- *Protein: 15.3 grams*
- *Fiber: 1.5 grams*

Stuffed Avocado Salmon GF

I love Salmon! Paired with Avocado and Salmon you are getting in a lot of Healthy Fats and your Omega Fatty acids.

Ingredients

6 skin-on salmon filets, about 2 pounds
1 avocado, pitted, peeled and thinly sliced
1 tablespoon olive oil
1/4 cup teriyaki sauce
2 1/2 cups cooked brown rice

1 Roma tomato diced
1 cup of black beans
3 green onions, chopped
1 tablespoon soy sauce
1 tablespoon rice wine vinegar
1 teaspoon sesame oil

Directions

Preheat oven to 400 F. Using a sharp paring knife, make a thin slit in the middle of each salmon filet, to form a pocket. Place 3 to 4 slices of avocado in each slit.

Heat a large oven proof sauté pan over medium high heat. Add olive oil and place salmon filets, skin side up and sauté 4 to 6 minutes or until golden brown.

Carefully flip over and drizzle with teriyaki sauce. Place pan in the oven for 8 to 10 minutes or until salmon is cooked through.

Meanwhile, heat cooked rice in a sauce pan over medium heat. Add tomatoes, black beans, green onion, soy sauce, rice wine vinegar and sesame oil and heat through until warm.

Serve each salmon filet with ½ cup wild rice salad.

Nutritional Information
- Calories: 388.6
- Fat: 16.6 grams
- Carbohydrates: 9 grams
- Protein: 48.3 grams
- Fiber: 0.3 grams

Cindy's Wheat Penne Turkey Casserole

Jason's New Favorite!

Ingredients

1 lb ground turkey
15 ozs tomato sauce
1 tsp stevia
8 ozs cottage cheese
8 ozs fat free cream cheese
12 ozs wheat penne noodles (uncooked)
2 cups mozzarella cheese
1 tbsp of Italian seasoning
1 tbsp of garlic powder
1 tsp sea salt
1 1/2 teaspoon black pepper
1 tsp of white pepper

Directions

Preheat oven to 350 degrees F (175 degrees C).
In a large skillet over medium-high heat, saute the ground turkey combining salt, garlic powder, pepper, white pepper, and Italian seasoning for 5 to 10 min., or until browned. Drain the turkey, stir in the tomato sauce and stevia, and set aside. In a medium bowl, combine the cottage cheese, cream cheese, 1 cup of mozzarella cheese . Mix well and set aside.
Cook noodles according to package directions. Place them into a 9x13-inch baking dish (coating with spray oil), then layer the turkey mixture over the noodles. Then layer the cream cheese mixture over the turkey, and top with remaining 1 cup of mozzarella cheese. Bake at 350 degrees F (175 degrees C) for 20 to 35 min., or until cheese is melted and bubbly.

Nutritional Information
- Calories: 353.9
- Fat: 7.9 grams
- Carbohydrates: 49.5 grams
- Protein: 27.1 grams
- Fiber: 6.8 grams

Roasted Cauliflower GF

A great side dish to add to any meal!

Ingredients

2 tablespoons minced garlic
3 tablespoons olive oil
1 large head cauliflower, separated into florets
1/3 cup grated Parmesan cheese
Kosher salt and black pepper to taste
1 tablespoon chopped fresh parsley

Directions

Preheat the oven to 450 degrees.
Grease a large casserole dish.
Place the olive oil and garlic in a large resealable bag.
Add cauliflower, and shake to mix.
Pour into the prepared casserole dish, and season with salt and pepper to taste.
Bake for 25 minutes, stirring halfway through.
Top with Parmesan cheese and parsley, and broil for 3 to 5 minutes, until golden brown.

Nutritional Information
- *Calories: 154.5*
- *Fat: 9.2 grams*
- *Carbohydrates: 15.9 grams*
- *Protein: 6.2 grams*
- *Fiber: 8.7 grams*

Stuffed Cream Cheese Chicken with Pecan Crust

Ready to impress your dinner guests with this recipe?

Ingredients

1 teaspoon of smart balance butter spread
8 ounces of fresh mushroom- sliced thin
6 ounces of Fat Free Cream Cheese, softened
6 thin skinless, boneless chicken breast
1 cup of stevia brown sugar blend
1/2 cup of Honey Dijon Mustard
1/2 cup of chopped pecans

Directions

Preheat oven 450 degrees. Melt butter in skillet over medium heat. Saute mushrooms until tender. While cooking combine in a small bowl your brown sugar and mustard. Reduce heat to low and stir in cream cheese until melted. Remove from heat. Coat a 9x13 baking dish with spray oil. On wax paper, lay out your chicken breast, spread with mushroom mixture and roll up. Lather mustard mixture over rolled chicken breast. Roll chicken in chopped nuts, place a tooth pick in breast and lay in baking dish. Bake in preheated oven for 15-20 min. or until juices run clean and chicken is no longer pink.

Nutritional Information
- *Calories: 192.7*
- *Fat: 7 grams*
- *Carbohydrates: 8.9 grams*
- *Protein: 23.1 grams*
- *Fiber: 0.7 grams*

Shrimp & Crab Enchiladas

If you are a seafood lover like myself, you will love this recipe

Ingredients

1 pack of Artisan Whole grain tortillas
8 oz shredded low fat cheddar cheese
8 oz crab meat drained
1 pound of cooked medium shrimp, deveined
20 oz of jalapeno salsa
8 oz of plain Greek yogurt
1/4 cup of green onions (chopped)
Sea Salt & Pepper to taste

Directions

Preheat oven to 350 degrees. Lay out tortillas on a flat surface. Mix the shrimp, crab meat, and cheese together in a bowl - leave some cheese for the topping. In the middle of each tortilla place filling, sprinkle with sea salt & pepper, and then roll up. You will be placing these side by side in a 9x13 glass cooking pan (spray cooking oil on pan). Pour jalapeno salsa on top. If you have remaining mixture, place on top of salsa. Sprinkle with remaining cheese. Cover with aluminum foil. Bake for 30 min., remove foil and bake uncovered for an additional 15 min. Top each one with Greek yogurt and green onions. I served with gluten free chips and homemade Guacamole.

Nutritional Information
- *Calories: 252*
- *Fat: 4.5 grams*
- *Carbohydrates: 35 grams*
- *Protein: 18.3 grams*
- *Fiber: 2.7 grams*

Cindy's Chicken Lo Mein ⓕ

Want an Asian dish without all the guilt.
Try this low fat, low sodium recipe!
Jason loved it!

Ingredients

4 boneless chicken breast cut into chunks
8 oz of gluten free spaghetti noodles
1 cup of sugar snap peas
2 medium carrots sliced into thin sticks
3 shallots (diced)
1 cup of thin sliced mushrooms
2 cups of fresh green beans
1 tbsp of olive oil
1 tbsp of fresh ginger (chopped)
1 tbsp of minced garlic
1/2 cup of low-sodium soy sauce
1/4 cup of rice vinegar

Directions

Cook pasta as directed. In a large skillet, saute shallots in olive oil over medium heat for a few minutes until soft. Add Chicken and cook until brown. Remove. Saute carrots and mushrooms for 3-5 min., then add snap peas and cook another few minutes.
Add chicken and green beans, and saute approx. 5 min. In a food processor, pulse remaining ingredients. Add to skillet and toss mixture until completely coated.
Turn the heat down to low, simmer for a few minutes. Serve over cooked noodles.

Nutritional Information
- *Calories: 241*
- *Fat: 11.8 grams*
- *Carbohydrates: 19.7 grams*
- *Protein: 6 grams*
- *Fiber: 1.4 grams*

Ground Turkey & Summer Squash Casserole ⓖⓕ

This was a very tasty meal, super fast and easy!
Right after we had dinner, Jason was asking me to make it again soon!
This is a great way to get in vegetables without the family complaining too much!

Ingredients

1 pound of ground turkey
1 tablespoon of olive oil/ canola oil
2 cups of yellow summer squash
1 yellow onion chopped
2 eggs
1 cup of almond milk
1 1/2 tablespoon of cornstarch
1 cup of shredded mozzarella cheese
6 tablespoons of smart balance butter, melted
1/2 teaspoon of sea salt
1/4 teaspoon pepper
1 cup of whole wheat bread crumbs

Directions

In a large skillet, cook turkey in oil over medium heat until no longer pink. Add the squash and onion. cook until vegetables are crispy.
In a small bowl, combine eggs, milk, cornstarch, cheese, butter, salt and pepper.
Stir into the turkey mixture. Transfer to a greased 8" square baking dish.
Sprinkle with bread crumbs.
Bake, uncovered, at 375 degrees for 35-40 min. or until heated through.

Nutritional Information
- Calories: 241.1
- Fat: 11.1 grams
- Carbohydrates: 17.6 grams
- Protein: 16.4 grams
- Fiber: 2.5 grams

Pan Seared Flounder Fillets

*I got some fresh wild caught flounder from Fresh Market,
first time cooking flounder.. these were YUMMY!
Along with the sale on flounder, stopped by Jimmy Lowe's fruit stand,
and picked up these Amish Made Tomato Basil Noodles*

Ingredients

4 skinless flounder-fillets
1 cup of almond milk
Sea salt & pepper to taste
1/2 cup of greek yogurt
Whole wheat flour for dredging fish

2 minced cloves of garlic
2 tablespoons of canola oil
4 tablespoons of smart balance butter spread, divided
1 lemon, squeezed
1 small bottle capers

Directions

Cook pasta as directed, I made a white creme sauce for this pasta. In a small sauce pan, on low/simmer heat together almond milk, butter, greek yogurt, garlic, and 1 tablespoon of butter. Add in salt & pepper for taste. Wash Fillets in cold water and pat dry, sprinkle with salt & pepper. Dredge fillets in flour. Place oil and 2 tablespoons butter in flat skillet on high heat until butter melts. Keeping heat at medium-high, cook fish on 1 side about 3 min., until deep brown and crispy. Turn fish and cook on second side, about 3 min. Turn fish only once. Remove fish to serving platter. Turn off heat. Into hot skillet, whisk remaining 1 tablespoon butter. Add lemon juice. Pour in capers , liquid and all. Whisk. Pour thin sauce over fish fillets. Serve with a side of pasta and veggies. Enjoy with a colorful salad!

Nutritional Information
- *Calories: 136*
- *Fat: 2.1 grams*
- *Carbohydrates: 6.1 grams*
- *Protein: 21.1 grams*
- *Fiber: 0.1 grams*

Chicken Adobo Lumpias

Ingredients

4 Thin sliced Chicken breasts- diced
1/4 cup of apple cider vinegar
2 tablespoons cup of low sodium soy sauce
4 cloves garlic, crushed and minced
2 bay leaves
1 tsp of baking stevia
1 tsp curshed black peppercorns
1 bunch chives
1 pkg large square spring rools
1 egg beaten
Canola oil for frying
Kosher salt
Greek yogurt for topping

Directions

In a pot, mix the diced chicken, viengar, soy sauce, garlic, bay leaves, stevia, and peppercorns. Place pot on stove, add enough water to cover chicken. Bring to a boil; lower the heat and simmer until chicken is nice and white. Transfer the chicken to a plate. Boil the sauce for about 5 min. and strain (set the sauce aside). In a food processor, pulse the chicken until finely chopped. Mix in the chives and 1/2 cup of sauce (reserve the other half for topping).
Lay out 1 wrapper on a clean surface. Spread with 2 heaping tablespoons of filling in thin line along one edge. Brush the opposite edge with the egg wash, fold in the edges and roll up tightly. Repeat, will make approx. 6 rolls.
In a medium skillet, heat 1 inch of oil med-high heat. Working the rolls until golden, approx. 2 min. each. Transfer to a paper towel to drain, sprinkle with Kosher salt. Cut Lupias in half and serve with a side of Greek Yogur*t*.

Nutritional Information
- *Calories: 45*
- *Fat: 2.4 grams*
- *Carbohydrates: 12 grams*
- *Protein: 5.8 grams*
- *Fiber: 0.9 grams*

Cindy's Version of Grilled Lamb Loin Chop with Roasted Mustard/Sage Sweet Potatoes, Mexican Mint Marigold Pesto and Warm Goat Cheese Sauce ⓖⓕ

This recipe was very elegant and not difficult at all to make! Found the recipe on Food Network, then I modified it to make it more healthy and less fattening!

Sweet Potatoes
Ingredients

1 tablespoon olive oil
3 tablespoons Dijon mustard
2 tablespoons honey (called for maple syrup)

1 tablespoon minced fresh sage leaves
1/4 teaspoon salt
1/8 teaspoon pepper
2 small sweet potatoes, peeled, cut into 1/4 - inch thick disks
Cooking spray

Pesto
Ingredients

1 tablespoon olive oil
3 tablespoons Dijon mustard
2 tablespoons honey (called for maple syrup)

1 tablespoon minced fresh sage leaves
1/4 teaspoon salt
1/8 teaspoon pepper
2 small sweet potatoes, peeled, cut into 1/4 - inch thick disks
Cooking spray

Nutritional Information
- Calories: 214
- Fat: 12.4 grams
- Carbohydrates: 1.1 grams
- Protein: 23.4 grams
- Fiber: 0.1 grams

see next page...

Cindy's Version of Grilled Lamb Loin Chop with Roasted Mustard/Sage Sweet Potatoes, Mexican Mint Marigold Pesto and Warm Goat Cheese Sauce

from previous page...

Goat Cheese Sauce

Ingredients

6 tablespoons chevre (goat cheese)
4 tablespoons almond milk (called for half & half)
1 tsp of cornstarch
Lamb: 4 (5 to 6-ounce) lamb loin chops
Salt
Pepper

Directions

Sweet Potatoes: Preheat the oven to 365 degrees F. Combine the first 6 ingredients. Toss with the sweet potatoes. Place the sweet potatoes in a single layer on a sprayed baking sheet. Roast for 20 to 25 min. until beginning to brown.
Pesto: Combine all ingredients in a food processor or blender and puree.
Goat Cheese Sauce: Combine the goat cheese and almond milk in a small saucepan and heat over low heat until goat cheese is melted and sauce is warm.
Lamb: Preheat a grill or grill pan over high heat. Season the lamb with the salt and pepper. Grill to desired doneness, about 3 min. per side for medium rare.
To serve, divide the sweet potatoes onto 4 plates, loosely stacking them towards the center. Position a lamb chop on each stack. Drizzle pesto around the potatoes. Spoon goat cheese sauce over lamb.

Nutritional Information
- *Calories: 178.2*
- *Fat: 7.5 grams*
- *Carbohydrates: 25.7 grams*
- *Protein: 2.3 grams*
- *Fiber: 3.9 grams*

Baked Costa Rican - Style Tilapia with Pineapples, Black Beans and Rice

This recipe was a hit at a small get together at our house!

Ingredients

1 cup Jasmine Rice
2 cups low-sodium chicken broth
1/4 cup freshly squeezed orange juice
1 lime, juiced
2 tablespoons olive oil
1/4 cup finely chopped fresh cilantro, plus more for garnish
2 garlic cloves, minced
1 teaspoon Stevia
Kosher salt and freshly ground black pepper
4 (5 to 7-ounce) tilapia fillets, rinsed and patted dry
2 cups jarred or homemade tomato salsa
1 (15-ounce) can black beans, drained and rinsed
2 cups diced fresh pineapple
2 limes, thinly sliced

Directions

Combine the rice and chicken broth in a pot over medium heat and bring to a boil. Reduce the heat to low, cover, and cook until the rice is tender and has absorbed all of the liquid, about 20 min. Preheat the oven to 400 degrees F. In a mixing bowl, whisk together the orange juice, lime juice, oil, 2 tablespoons of the cilantro, the garlic, and sugar; season with salt and pepper. Add the tilapia fillets to the marinade, turning to coat. Marinate in the refrigerator for 20 min., turning occasionally. Stir together the cooked rice, salsa, beans, pineapple, and remaining 2 tablespoons of the cilantro in a 2 or 3-quart baking dish. Remove the tilapia from the marinade, reserve the marinade, and lay the fish fillets over the rice mixture, overlapping if necessary. Pour the reserved marinade over the fish. Shingle the lime slices over the fish. Bake until the fish flakes easily, is opaque, and cooked through, 25 to 30 min. Garnish with chopped cilantro before serving.

Nutritional Information
- *Calories: 288.1*
- *Fat: 5.7 grams*
- *Carbohydrates: 57.8 grams*
- *Protein: 37.8 grams*
- *Fiber: 4.6 grams*

Vegetable Meatloaf

This recipe is quick and easy and the whole family will love it!

Ingredients

2 tablespoons extra-virgin olive oil
1 small zucchini, finely diced
1 red bell pepper, finely diced
1 yellow bell pepper, finely diced
5 cloves garlic, minced
1/2 teaspoon red pepper flakes
Kosher salt and freshly ground pepper
1 large egg, lightly beaten
1 tablespoon finely chopped fresh thyme
1/4 cup chopped fresh parsley
1 1/2 pounds ground turkey (90 percent lean)
1 cup quick oats oatmeal
1/2 cup freshly grated Romano or Parmesan cheese
3/4 cup ketchup
1/4 cup plus 2 tablespoons balsamic vinegar

Directions

Preheat the oven to 425 degrees. Heat the oil in a large saute pan over high heat. Add the zucchini, bell peppers, garlic paste and 1/4 teaspoon red pepper flakes. Season with salt and pepper and cook until the vegetables are almost soft, about 5 minutes. Set aside to cool. Whisk the egg and fresh herbs in a large bowl. Add the turkey, quick oats oatmeal, grated cheese, 1/2 cup ketchup, 2 tablespoons balsamic vinegar and the cooled vegetables; mix until just combined. Gently press the mixture into a 9-by-5-inch loaf pan. Whisk the remaining 1/4 cup ketchup, 1/4 cup balsamic vinegar and 1/4 teaspoon red pepper flakes in a small bowl; brush the mixture over the entire loaf. Bake for 1 to 1 1/4 hours. Let rest for 10 min. before slicing.

Nutritional Information
- Calories: 247.2
- Fat: 13.5 grams
- Carbohydrates: 12.9 grams
- Protein: 17.4 grams
- Fiber: 0.8 grams

Pork Chops with Hickory Smoked Turkey Bacon (GF)

Not only will the house smell amazing when you are cooking this recipe, but it will be a hit at the dinner table.

Ingredients

4 pork chops
olive oil
2 onions sliced in rings
chicken-porkherb rub to taste
Seasoned Salt to taste
Coarsely ground pepper to taste
paprika
4 hickory smoked turkey bacon slices

Directions

Cover bottom of dutch oven with olive oil, about 1/4 cup. Place slices of one onion over oil. Sprinkle onions with paprika. Then sprinkle with herb rub. Then sprinkle with pepper. Arrange pork chops on top of this. Sprinkle chops with Seasoned Salt. Sprinkle then with herb rub. Place rings of second onion over seasoned chops. Place bacon slices over onions. Sprinkle top generously with paprika and pepper. Bake covered in a 300 degree oven for about 1 hour and 25 min. Remove from oven and make gravy with the drippings.

Nutritional Information
- Calories: 220.8
- Fat: 11.7 grams
- Carbohydrates: 1 grams
- Protein: 25.7 grams
- Fiber: 0 grams

Sicilian-Style Tuna GF

*A great way to mix up a traditional tuna steak!
Packed full of flavor and spices! Making healthy taste good!*

Ingredients

- 6 tablespoons extra-virgin olive oil
- 4 (5- to 6-ounce) tuna steaks
- Salt and freshly ground black pepper
- 1 large onion, sliced (about 1 cup)
- 2 garlic cloves, minced
- 3 tablespoons salted capers, soaked in water for 10 minutes and drained
- 3 tablespoons minced pitted green olives
- 1/4 cup raisins
- 5 plum tomatoes, peeled, seeded, and chopped
- 1 cup fish stock or water, as needed
- 2 tablespoons fresh flat-leaf parsley, coarsely chopped
- 4 to 5 fresh basil leaves, torn
- 1/3 cup pine nuts, toasted

Directions

In a medium skillet over moderately high heat, warm the oil. Season the tuna with salt and pepper and sauté, turning once, until golden on both sides, 3 to 4 min. total. Remove the tuna and set aside. Do not clean the pan. In the same pan over low heat, sauté the onion, stirring frequently, until just tender, about 1 minute. Add the garlic, capers, olives, raisins, and tomatoes, and continue cooking, stirring, until heated through, about 2 min. If the tomatoes don't release much juice, add the fish stock or water to give the sauce some body. Return the tuna to the pan and cover it with a tight-fitting lid. Cook over moderate heat until the tuna reaches the desired doneness, 2 to 3 min. for medium. Add the parsley and basil and stir to incorporate, then season to taste with salt and pepper. Serve the fish with the sauce spooned over the top; garnish with pine nuts.

Nutritional Information
- *Calories: 298.8*
- *Fat: 7 grams*
- *Carbohydrates: 21.5 grams*
- *Protein: 28.9 grams*
- *Fiber: 2.2 grams*

Cumin Crusted Swordfish with Avocado Relish

This is one of my favorite fish dishes! Yummy!

Avocado Relish

Ingredients

- 1 small avocado, peeled, seeded and finely chopped
- 1/2 cup coarsely chopped tomato
- 1/4 cup finely chopped red onion
- 2 tablespoons chopped fresh cilantro
- 2 tablespoons olive oil
- 1 tablespoon lime juice
- 1/2 tablespoon Red Pepper, Crushed
- 1/8 teaspoon Sea Salt

Cumin-Crusted Swordfish

Ingredients

- 1 tablespoon Coriander Seed, coarsely crushed
- 1/2 teaspoon Black Pepper, Cracked
- 1 tablespoon Cumin
- 1/2 teaspoon Sea Salt
- 3 swordfish steaks, about 1-inch thick (8 ounces each), skin removed

Directions

For the Avocado Relish, mix all ingredients in medium bowl. Set aside. Mix coriander, cumin, pepper and sea salt in small bowl. Cut each swordfish steak into 2 pieces. Brush swordfish with oil. Rub seasoning mixture evenly over swordfish. Grill over medium heat 5 to 7 min. per side or until fish flakes easily with a fork. Serve swordfish topped with Avocado Relish.

Nutritional Information
- Calories: 242.5
- Fat: 12.6 grams
- Carbohydrates: 3.6 grams
- Protein: 27.4 grams
- Fiber: 0.9 grams

Quinoa with Chard & Pine Nuts

A great side dish to add in at lunch, dinner, or eat alone for added fiber.

Ingredients

1 1/2 cups low-sodium vegetable broth
3/4 cup quinoa, rinsed and drained
2 tsp. olive oil
1 lb. Swiss chard, leaves cut into ribbons, stems finely chopped
1 medium yellow onion, chopped (1 ½ cups)
16 pitted black olives
1/4 cup of raisins
1/2 tsp. red pepper flakes
3 cloves garlic, minced (1 Tbs.)
2 Tbs. toasted pine nuts

Directions

Bring broth to a boil in medium saucepan. Add quinoa, and bring mixture to a simmer. Reduce heat to medium-low, and simmer, covered, 12 min. Remove from heat, uncover, let stand 5 minutes, then fluff with fork.
Meanwhile, heat oil in large nonstick skillet over medium heat.
Add chard stems, onion, olives, and raisins.
Sauté 10 min., or until onion and chard stems are soft. Stir in chard leaves and red pepper flakes; sauté 6 min., or until greens are tender.
Stir in garlic, and season with salt and pepper, if desired. Divide quinoa among 4 shallow bowls. Spoon chard mixture over top, and sprinkle with pine nuts.

Nutritional Information
- Calories: 294.9
- Fat: 13.1 grams
- Carbohydrates: 38.4 grams
- Protein: 7.4 grams
- Fiber: 5.4 grams

Roasted Chicken Drumsticks & Red Potatoes with Mojo Sauce

This meal is super cheap to make, easy to prepare, and tastes amazing!

Goat Cheese Sauce

Ingredients

5 Chicken drumsticks (skin removed)
1 pound red potatoes (leave whole and wash)
2 tablespoons of canola oil
1 teaspoon of sea salt (divided)
1/2 teaspoon freshly ground pepper
2/3 cup of fresh squeezed orange juice
3 tablespoons of fresh squeezed lime juice
1/4 cup chopped fresh cilantro
5 cloves of garlic
1 teaspoon of ground cumin
1 teaspoon onion powder
1/2 teaspoon of dried oregano

Directions

Preheat oven to 475 degrees. Line a large baking sheet with heavy duty aluminum foil and spray with cooking spray. Toss chicken and potatoes in a large bowl with 1 tablespoon oil, 1/2 teaspoon salt and 1/4 teaspoon pepper: layout in single layer on cooking sheet. Bake, turning once halfway through and thermometer reads 165 (30-35 min.) While that is baking in the oven, combine orange juice, lime juice, 2 tablespoons cilantro, garlic, cumin, onion powder, oregano, the remaining tablespoon of oil, 1/2 teaspoon of salt, 1/4 teaspoon of pepper in a blender or food processor. Transfer to a small saucepan: bring to a boil over medium-high heat, reduce heat and maintain a simmer, continue to cook for 8-10 min. Serve each portion of chicken and potatoes with 2 tablespoons of sauce. I served this with organic green beans, tossed with a lemon zest and sliced almonds.

Nutritional Information
- *Calories: 394.6*
- *Fat: 18.6 grams*
- *Carbohydrates: 37.2 grams*
- *Protein: 20.3 grams*
- *Fiber: 4.7 grams*

Lemon Zest Green Beans

Ingredients

2 pounds green beans, ends trimmed
1 tablespoon extra-virgin olive oil
3 tablespoons smart balance butter
2 large garlic cloves, minced
1 tablespoon lemon zest
Salt and freshly ground black pepper
1/3 cup of sliced almonds

Directions

Blanch green beans in a large stock pot of well salted boiling water until bright green in color and tender crisp, roughly 2 min. Drain and shock in a bowl of ice water to stop from cooking. Heat a large heavy skillet over medium heat.

Add the oil and the butter. Add the garlic and red pepper flakes and saute until fragrant, about 30 seconds. Add the beans and continue to saute until coated in the butter and heated through, about 5 min. Add lemon zest and season with salt and pepper.

Nutritional Information
- Calories: 124.6
- Fat: 7.5 grams
- Carbohydrates: 13 grams
- Protein: 3.9 grams
- Fiber: 5.3 grams

Grilled Cobia GF

This is a very mild fish and can be prepared many ways.
They say it's one of the best tasting fishes, I would have to agree. The pork chop of the sea.
One thing I am learning is not to overdue the spices which would block out the fish taste.
This recipe has good flavor, yet you can savor the fish itself.

Ingredients

4-5 medium fillets Cobia
1/3 cup olive oil
1/3 cup lemon juice
2 teaspoons dry mustard powder
1 clove minced garlic
1 teaspoon celery seed
1/2 teaspoon pepper
1/2 teaspoon sea salt
1 1/2 cup of white wine

Directions

Mix all ingredients in a freezer ziploc bag and place in refridgerator.
Marinate for an hour.
Grill on Medium Heat either using outside grill or grill plate. Turning several times, and baste with extra marinade at each turn. Don't over cook. Super easy recipe.
Paired with Raw Zucchini, Garlic Cabbage, & left over Couscous.

Nutritional Information
- *Calories: 368.3*
- *Fat: 17 grams*
- *Carbohydrates: 5.6 grams*
- *Protein: 40.5 grams*
- *Fiber: 1.5 grams*

Almond Encrusted Yellow Tail Fish ⓖⓕ

This is a great summer dish! Your whole family will love it!

Ingredients

2 servings
3 8 oz. yellow tail snapper fillets
1/4 tsp. sea salt & pepper
1 lemon juiced
1 c. almond flour
1 egg
1/2 c. almond milk
1 c. chopped sliced almonds
4 tsp. canola
3 tsp. Smart Balance butter spread
1/4 c. dry white wine

Directions

Season yellow tail fillets with salt, pepper and lemon juice, then dredge in almond milk, almond flour and egg wash. Coat fillets in chopped almonds. Pat the almonds on the fish to secure. Saute in canola oil over medium heat, taking care not to burn almonds, until nicely browned. Remove fillets and de-glaze pan with splash of white wine. Add a squeeze of lemon and melt butter in pan juices. Drizzle over fish and garnish with lemon slices and parsley.

Nutritional Information
- Calories: 240.8
- Fat: 7.2 grams
- Carbohydrates: 4.8 grams
- Protein: 38.6 grams
- Fiber: 0.5 grams

Baked Chicken

*Clients are always asking me the best way to prepare chicken, especially if they are meal prepping.
This is easy and tastes amazing!*

Ingredients

2 tablespoons of olive oil
1 clove minced garlic
1 cup of wheat bread crumbs
2/3 cup grated Parmesan
1 teaspoon dried basil leaves
1/4 teaspoon ground black pepper
6 skinless, boneless chicken breast halves

Directions

Preheat oven to 350 degrees.
Lightly grease a 9 x 13 baking dish
In a bowl, blend the olive oil and garlic. In a separate bowl, mix the bread crumbs, Parmesan cheese, basil, and pepper. Dip each chicken breast in the oil mixture, then in the bread crumb mixture. Arrange the coated chicken breasts in the prepared baking dish, and top with any remaining bread crumb mixture. Bake 30 min. in the preheated oven, or until chicken is no longer pink and juices run clear.

Nutritional Information
- *Calories: 168.1*
- *Fat: 4.9 grams*
- *Carbohydrates: 2.2 grams*
- *Protein: 26.5 grams*
- *Fiber: 0.5 grams*

Grilled Honey Dijon Sesame Seed Tuna Steak

*This is a twist on the traditional tuna steak.
If you are still getting accustomed to eating fish, this is a great recipe without the fishy flavor.*

Ingredients

2 Tuna Steaks
2 Tablespoons of Honey Dijon Mustard
1 tablespoon of sesame seeds
Sea salt & Black Pepper for taste

Directions

Preheat your grill or grill plate - Med to High heat. Pat your tuna steaks dry with a paper towel. Brush on the honey Dijon mustard on one side. Sprinkle on the sesame seeds.
Salt and Pepper. Using a fork, place on to the grill mustard side down. Once on the grill, repeat the steps to the side facing up. Sear your tuna steak for 2-3 min. on each side.

Benefits of tuna fish
A 3-ounce serving of cooked yellow fin tuna provides 25 grams protein, or 50 percent of the daily value based on a 2,000-calorie diet, and it contains only 110 calories. Choosing tuna for your protein source instead of fatty meats, such as red meat, can save calories and help you control your weight.

Nutritional Information
- Calories: 205.7
- Fat: 1.4 grams
- Carbohydrates: 16.5 grams
- Protein: 32.6 grams
- Fiber: 1.6 grams

Green Beans with Almonds and Thyme ⓖⓕ

Always a crowd pleaser, turning the basic green bean dish into a gourmet cuisine.

Ingredients

2 lbs of (fresh or frozen) green beans, trimmed
1/4 cup (1/2 stick) butter- smart balance
1 Tbsp Dijon mustard
1 teaspoon garlic salt
2 Tbsp chopped fresh thyme
1/3 cup slivered almonds, lightly toasted

Directions

Cook the green beans in a large pot of boiling salted water until just crisp-tender, about 5 minutes. Drain the beans and transfer them to a large bowl of ice water, cooling them completely. (The ice water will shock the beans into a vibrant green color.) Drain the beans well. At this point you can make the beans a day ahead and store in refrigerator. Alternatively you can steam the beans for 5 min. and proceed directly to the skillet. Melt the butter in a large, heavy skillet over medium high heat. Whisk in half of the fresh thyme (1 Tbsp), the Dijon mustard and garlic salt into the butter. Add the beans to the skillet and toss until heated through, about 4 min. Transfer to a serving bowl. Sprinkle with toasted almonds and the remaining 1 Tbsp of thyme.

Nutritional Information
- *Calories: 78*
- *Fat: 4.4 grams*
- *Carbohydrates: 8.5 grams*
- *Protein: 2.6 grams*
- *Fiber: 3.4 grams*

Cuban Picadillo GF

I came up with the recipe out of my husbands love for Cuban food!

Ingredients

2 tbsps olive oil
1 white onion (yellow, finely chopped about 1 cup)
1 red bell pepper (cored and seeded finely chopped about 34 cup)
1 tbsp tomato paste
4 cloves clove garlic (finely chopped about 4 teaspoons)
2 tsps ground cumin
2 tsps dried oregano
kosher salt
black pepper
2 bay leaves
1/2 cup red wine
11/2 lbs ground turkey
1 cup canned tomatoes (diced)
2 tbsps worcestershire sauce
1/3 cup raisins
8 oz of red potatoes peeled and cubed

Directions

Heat oil in large skillet over medium-high heat until shimmering. Add onion and bell pepper and cook, stirring occasionally, until softened, 5 to 7 min. Add tomato paste, garlic, cumin, oregano, 1 1/2 teaspoons salt, 1 teaspoon pepper, and bay leaves and cook until fragrant and tomato paste darkens in color, about 2 min. Add wine and cook until reduced to 1/4 cup, about 5 min. Add meat and cook, stirring and breaking up chunks, until no longer pink, 5 to 7 minutes. Stir in tomatoes, Worcestershire sauce, raisins, and potatoes. Cover, reduce heat to medium-low, and cook until potatoes are tender, about 12 min. Remove cover and season to taste with salt and pepper. Remove and discard bay leaves. Serve with yellow rice and black beans.

Nutritional Information
- *Calories: 225.4*
- *Fat: 9.5 grams*
- *Carbohydrates: 15.9 grams*
- *Protein: 19.9 grams*
- *Fiber: 2.3 grams*

Cindy's Sautéed Mint Salmon GF DF

*This is definitely my most favorite fish dish!
I was playing around with just a few items while visiting California
with my parnter and friend Heather Harp and made her this recipe.
I instantly fell in love! Memories of California!*

Ingredients

4 Salmon Filets with no skin
1 shallot finely chopped
1 tablespoon fresh mint chopped
1/3 cup of olive oil
1 lemon
1 tsp of fresh ground pepper
1 tsp of sea salt
1 packet of stevia

Directions

In a small bowl pour 1/3 cup of olive oil.
1 tsp of lemon zest. 2 tbsp of lemon juice.
Add the mint, pepper, sea salt, stevia and set to the side.
On med-high heat use remaining olive oil and Sautee the shallots.
On a plate salt and pepper both sides of the salmon filets.
Add the filets to the pan and cook 4-5 min. on each side, then top with sauce.

Nutritional Information
- Calories: 236
- Fat: 9.3 grams
- Carbohydrates: 7.9 grams
- Protein: 29.3 grams
- Fiber: 1.1 grams

Brussel Sprouts (GF) (DF) (V)

This is definitely my favorite vegetable!

Ingredients

3 tbsp of extra-virgin olive oil
1 pint brussels sprouts (1 pound total), trimmed and halved lengthwise
Sea salt and ground pepper
1/2 lemon fresh lemon juice

Directions

In a large skillet, heat oil over medium-high.
Add brussels sprouts, season with salt and pepper, and cook, stirring frequently, until caramelized, 8 to 10 minutes.
Add 1/4 cup water and cook until evaporated, about 2 minutes.
Add lemon juice and toss to coat. Serve immediately.

Nutritional Information
- Calories: 112.4
- Fat: 1.3 grams
- Carbohydrates: 4.9 grams
- Protein: 1.5 grams
- Fiber: 1.7 grams

Spinach Stuffed Chicken Breasts ⓖⒻ

Ingredients

1 (10 ounce) package fresh spinach leaves
1/2 cup Greek yogurt
1/2 cup shredded mozzarella cheese
4 cloves garlic, minced
4 skinless, boneless chicken breast halves - pounded to 1/2 inch thickness
1/2 tsp ground black pepper
1/2 tsp of garlic powder
1 tsp sea salt

Directions

Preheat the oven to 375 degrees F (190 degrees C).
Place spinach in a large glass bowl, and heat in the microwave for 3 minutes, stirring every minute or so, or until wilted.
Stir in Greek yogurt, mozzarella cheese, pepper, sea salt, and garlic.
Lay the chicken breasts out on a clean surface, and spoon some of the spinach mixture onto each one. Roll up chicken to enclose the spinach mixture. Secure with toothpicks, and arrange in a shallow baking dish. Sprinkle garlic powder on top. Bake uncovered for 35 min. in the preheated oven.

Nutritional Information
- Calories: 403.5
- Fat: 12.7 grams
- Carbohydrates: 10.1 grams
- Protein: 60.2 grams
- Fiber: 3 grams

Ground Turkey Sweet Potato Casserole

Ingredients

1 tbsp Enzo Basil Olive Oil
1/2 onion (diced)
1 red bell pepper (diced)
3 cloves garlic (minced)
1 lb ground turkey
1 tsp dried oregano
1 tsp dried parsley
1/2 tsp fennel seeds
1/4 tsp red pepper flakes
2 tbsp fresh basil (chopped)
14.5 oz can diced tomatoes
3 small sweet potatoes
8 oz fresh mozzarella cheese (sliced)

Directions

Preheat oven to 350 degrees. Add olive oil to a large skillet over medium-high heat. Saute bell pepper and onion for 3-5 min. Add garlic, saute for 1-2 min. Add the ground turkey and cook through. Place the oregano, parsley, fennel seeds and red pepper flakes in a spice grinder (or use a mortal and pestle to grind by hand.) Add the ground herbs to the turkey. Add the fresh basil and diced tomatoes. Reduce the heat to low and simmer for 15 min. In the mean time, get spiralizing! Slice the ends off of the sweet potatoes, peel, cut in half and spiralize with Blade. Add the spiralized sweet potatoes to the skillet. Toss and cook for 3-5 min. If the skillet is not oven safe, transfer the casserole to an oven-safe dish and top with the fresh mozzarella cheese. If the dish you are using on the skillet is oven safe, simply top with the fresh mozzarella and in the oven it goes... there's where that whole "One Dish Meal" thing comes in! Garnish with a little more fresh basil if you would like! If you're looking for a paleo or non-dairy dinner, simply omit the mozzarella. I made a small dish without the cheese and it turned out great as well!

Nutritional Information
- Calories: 230.7
- Fat: 7 grams
- Carbohydrates: 25.5 grams
- Protein: 19.8 grams
- Fiber: 8.2 grams

Healthy Snacks to munch on while sitting at your desk!

Greek Yogurt - THE GOOD NEWS: Greek yogurt is a great source of calcium, protein and probiotics (which is good for your digestive system). SNACK TIP: Mix berries or granola with a cup of sugar-free Greek yogurt

Trail Mix - THE GOOD NEWS: Eaten in portions, homemade trail mix can be packed with fiber. SNACK TIP: For kids, Make a homemade trail mix with seeds and dried fruits (avoid nuts because of allergies) and for yourself, add in popcorn or even whole wheat pretzels.

Apple and Peanut Butter - THE GOOD NEWS: Apples can boost your immune system and natural peanut butter is full of protein. SNACK TIP: Dip sliced apple pieces in plain Cheerios for a crunchy snack.

Edamame - THE GOOD NEWS: Edamame is full of protein and fiber. SNACK TIP: Buy frozen edamame beans and keep them in your office freezer. Pop them in the microwave and add cherry tomatoes for a quick and wholesome snack.

Cucumbers and Low-Fat Cheese - THE GOOD NEWS: Cucumber is packed with vitamin K (needed for strong bones) and low-fat cheese is full of calcium. SNACK TIP: Make mini cucumber sandwiches by taking low-fat cheese and turkey and wedging them in between two slices of cucumbers - the kids will also love this one.

H₂O

We need it! How much do we need to drink daily? Which kind is better for us? And most important the benefits!

Health benefits of water according to the *Mayo Clinic*. Functions of water in the body. Water is your body's principal chemical component and makes up about 60 percent of your body weight. Every system in your body depends on water. For example, water flushes toxins out of vital organs, carries nutrients to your cells and provides a moist environment for ear, nose and throat tissues. Lack of water can lead to dehydration, a condition that occurs when you don't have enough water in your body to carry out normal functions. Even mild dehydration can drain your energy and make you tired.

How much water do you need? Every day you lose water through your breath, perspiration, urine and bowel movements. For your body to function properly, you must replenish its water supply by consuming beverages and foods that contain water. So how much fluid does the average, healthy adult living in a temperate climate need? *The Institute of Medicine* determined that an adequate intake (AI) for men is roughly 3 liters (about 13 cups) of total beverages a day. The AI for women is 2.2 liters (about 9 cups) of total beverages a day.

Drinking water for weight loss! Despite the fact that most diets call for drinking at least eight, 8-ounce glasses of water a day, few studies have been done to determine if the practice actually speeds weight loss. In an effort to answer this question, Michael Boschmann, MD, and colleagues from *Berlin's Franz-Volhard Clinical Research Center* tracked energy expenditures among seven men and seven women who were healthy and not overweight. After drinking approximately 17 ounces of water, the subjects' metabolic rates - or the rate at which calories are burned - increased by 30% for both men and women. The increases occurred within 10 minutes of water consumption and reached a maximum after about 30 to 40 minutes.
The study also showed that the increase in metabolic rate differed in men and women. In men, burning more fat fueled the increase in metabolism, whereas in women, an increased breakdown of carbohydrates caused the increase in metabolism seen. The researchers estimate that over the course of a year, a person who increases his water consumption by 1.5 liters a day would burn an extra 17,400 calories, for a weight loss of approximately five pounds. They note that up to 40% of the increase in calorie burning is caused by the body's attempt to heat the ingested water. The findings are reported in the December issue of *The Journal of Clinical Endocrinology and Metabolism.*

Which bottled water is best? VOSS, Fiji, Evian

Healthy Snacks for a Busy Summer

It's that time of year and school is out and your summer schedule is packed!
A client asked me for some tips on healthy summer snacks on the go. We want to make sure we get in nutritious healthy snacks for ourselves and our kids loaded with Protein and complex carbohydrates to prevent spikes in insulin levels.

Fruit and Yogurt Parfait - You can make these yourself or you can get them mostly any fast food restaurant, starbucks etc. We will use frozen berries layered with greek yogurt. You are getting a protein packed snack with 1 serving of fruit.

Protein Smoothie - We have made these in the past, these are great to make yourself or you can find low fat, low sugar, high protein smoothies around town at places like Tropical Smoothie, Smoothie King, City Blends.

Apple & Almonds - Super easy to pack- just toss in your bag and head out the door.

Rice Cake with Yogurt & Fruit - This is one of my favorites! We use the Caramel Corn flavored rice cake, topped with a layer of greek yogurt and sliced strawberries - YUM!

Rice Cake with Peanut Butter - This is another favorite, especially amongst my trainers. You are getting a super easy quick snack loaded with Protein that will keep you feeling full for hours!

DESSERTS

"Would you rather be covered in sweat at the gym or covered in clothes at the beach?"

Cindy's Healthy Pumpkin Cheesecake Bars

Because of the pumpkin, these are super high in fiber and will keep you full for a long time!

Ingredients

6 tablespoons smart balance butter melted and cooled
1 3/4 cups stevia
3 large eggs
1 1/2 teaspoon pure vanilla extract
1 cup canned pure pumpkin
1/3 cup water
1 3/4 cups all-purpose wheat flour
1 tablespoon pumpkin pie spice
1 teaspoon baking soda
1/2 teaspoon baking powder
1/2 kosher salt
1 package (8 oz.) fat free or lite cream cheese, at room temperature

Directions

Preheat oven to 350°. Line a 10x15 inch baking pan with non-stick foil or parchment paper and spray with non-stick cooking spray. In a bowl, with an electric mixer on medium speed, beat butter and 1 1/2 cups stevia until smooth. Beat in 2 eggs, pumpkin, 1 teaspoon of vanilla and 1/3 cup water until well blended. In another bowl, mix flour, pumpkin pie spice, baking soda, baking powder, and salt; add the dry ingredients into the butter mixture until and combine until well blended. Spread batter evenly into the prepared pan. In a bowl, with an electric mixer on medium speed, beat cream cheese, remaining egg, remaining 1/4 cup sugar, and remaining 1/2 teaspoon of vanilla until smooth. Drop cream cheese mixture in evenly spaced portions over the pumpkin batter. Pull a knife tip through filling to swirl slightly into batter. Bake in a 350° oven until center of the pumpkin batter (not cream cheese mixture) springs back when touched, about 30 minutes. Let cool completely in pan, then cut into 24 bars.

Nutritional Information
- Calories: 113.4
- Fat: 4.8 grams
- Carbohydrates: 15.3 grams
- Protein: 22.9 grams
- Fiber: 2 grams

Homemade Protein Bars

Why buy the processed bars with all the sugar alcohols when you can make your own for half the cost!

Ingredients

1/2 cup of Natural Jiff Peanut Butter
1/3 cup of honey
1 tablespoon of Agave Nectar
1/4 cup of coconut oil
1 1/2 cup of Old fashioned oats
1 1/2 tablespoons wheat germ
1/2 scoop of chocolate whey protein powder
1/2 cup of ground flax seed
1/4 cup of dry roasted peanuts
1/4 cup of dark chocolate chips

Directions

Melt peanut butter, honey and coconut oil together in a small sauce pan over low/medium heat, stirring constantly. It only takes a minute or two to melt. In mixing bowl, combine all other ingredients except for chocolate chips, and stir well. Pour liquid mixture over dry mixture and stir until well combined. Let cool in bowl for several minutes. Place mixture into foil lined 8x8 pan and press down firmly. Sprinkle chocolate chips over top and press down firmly with hands. Place in Fridge or Freezer to set. Flip the foil out onto cutting board and cut into desired bar sizes. Makes 12-14 bars.

Nutritional Information
- Calories: 206.7
- Fat: 8.2 grams
- Carbohydrates: 22.3 grams
- Protein: 12.3 grams
- Fiber: 3.6 grams

Oatmeal/Banana/Peanut Butter Protein Squares

These are so good, you won't even know they are good for you!

Ingredients

1 & 1/2 cups of old fashioned oats
1/4 cup of stevia/brown sugar blend
1 teaspoon of baking powder
1/2 teaspoon of sea salt
1 teaspoon of cinnamon
1 teaspoon of vanilla extract
1/2 cup of almond milk
1 Large mashed banana
1 large egg, lightly beaten
1/4 cup of creamy natural Jiff peanut butter

Directions

Mix together the oats, brown sugar, baking powder, salt, and cinnamon. Add in the vanilla extract, milk, and egg. Mix the ingredients together. Add in the mashed banana and peanut butter. Mix the ingredients together.
Pour the mixture into a lightly greased 8x8 baking pan.
Bake at 350 degrees for 20 min.
Cool and cut into squares. Makes 12-14 squares.

Nutritional Information
- Calories: 125.5
- Fat: 5.5 grams
- Carbohydrates: 15.9 grams
- Protein: 15.5 grams
- Fiber: 2.6 grams

Pumpkin Chocolate Chip Muffins

Two things here, pumpkin and dark chocolate!
Both great for you and when combined, you are getting a healthy treat!

Ingredients

4 eggs
2 cups of baking Stevia
1 (15 ounce) can pumpkin
1 teaspoon vanilla extract
1 1/4 cups of canola oil
3 cups of flour (I used almond flour)
2 teaspoons baking soda
2 teaspoons baking powder
2 teaspoons cinnamon
1 teaspoon sea salt
12 ounces dark chocolate chips (I like the mini ones better)

Directions

In a large mixing bowl beat eggs, stevia, pumpkin, vanilla, and oil until smooth.
Mix dry ingredients together and mix into pumpkin mixture. Fold in chocolate chips.
Fill greased or paper lined muffin cups full.
Bake at 400 degrees for 16-20 min. Makes 24 muffins.

Nutritional Information
- Calories: 174.6
- Fat: 6.7 grams
- Carbohydrates: 32.5 grams
- Protein: 2.2 grams
- Fiber: 1.5 grams

Chocolate/Peanut Butter/Banana Ice Cream (GF) (DF) (V)

Ok guys... Here is my homemade healthy ice cream!

Ingredients

1 1/2 peeled medium bananas, sliced into coins and frozen until solid
3 tablespoons natural peanut butter
2 teaspoons honey
2 Tbsp dark cocoa powder
1 tbsp of chocolate protein powder
1 tbsp of almond milk
1/2 tbsp vanilla extract

Directions

Blend bananas in food processor until they are the consistency of soft serve ice cream. Blend in peanut butter, dark cocoa powder, almond milk, vanilla extract, and honey. Transfer to a freezer container and freeze until solid.

Nutritional Information
- Calories: 145.7
- Fat: 4.7 grams
- Carbohydrates: 25.9 grams
- Protein: 5.5 grams
- Fiber: 1.2 grams

Low Sugar Chocolate Chip Cookies

Two things here, pumpkin and dark chocolate!
Both great for you and when combined, you are getting a healthy treat!

Ingredients

2 1/2 cups whole wheat flour
2 eggs
1 teaspoon vanilla extract
3/4 teaspoon sea salt
1 teaspoon baking soda
6 ounces dark chocolate chips
1 cup of baking stevia

2 tablespoons honey
1 1/4 cup - I can't believe its not butter - original

Directions

Pre heat oven to 375 degrees F. Cream the butter with the stevia and the honey. Stir in the eggs and vanilla. Add the flour and baking soda. Stir in chocolate chips. Place teaspoon sized dough about 2 inches apart on an ungreased baking sheet. Bake at 375 degrees for 10 min. or until golden brown.
Makes 36 cookies (34 Calories/cookie).

Nutritional Information
- Calories: 41.8
- Fat: 1.7 grams
- Carbohydrates: 6.5 grams
- Protein: 0.7 grams
- Fiber: 0.4 grams

Almond Butter Balls

Ingredients

1/2 cup of Almond Butter
1 cup of Confection Sugar- (I use baking Stevia)
1 tbsp of milk (I use skim milk or almond milk)
1 tbsp of cocoa powder (I use a chocolate flavored protein powder)
1 tbsp of vanilla extract

Directions

Mix together 1/2 cup almond butter, 1/2 cup of confection sugar, cocoa powder, milk, and vanilla extract. Roll into quarter size balls. On a sheet of wax paper have the other 1/2 cup of confection sugar laid out. Roll the almond butter balls around on the paper until covered completely. You can serve as is, or put into the fridge and serve cold.
Nutrition: Each ball is 7 grams of protein and 45 calories.

Nutritional Information
- Calories: 126.5
- Fat: 8.5 grams
- Carbohydrates: 12.1 grams
- Protein: 2.8 grams
- Fiber: 1.2 grams

Raw Avocado Mousse GF DF V

Ingredients

4 Ripe Avocados
2 tsp of honey
1/2 cup of unsweetened cocoa powder
1 teaspoon of vanilla extract
Pinch of salt
Fresh fruit or nuts for garnish

Directions

In the bowl of a blender or food processor, blend avocado until smooth. Add all the other ingredients, blending until mixture is smooth. Chill for about 2 hours in the fridge or half an hour in the freezer.
Garnish with fresh fruit or chopped nuts.

Nutritional Information
- Calories: 187.8
- Fat: 14.8 grams
- Carbohydrates: 14.1 grams
- Protein: 3.8 grams
- Fiber: 9.5 grams

Cheesecake Stuffed Strawberries

This is a crowd pleaser for sure, without all the guilt!

Ingredients

1 lb large strawberries
1 (8 ounce) package cream cheese, softened
1/4 - 1/2 cup powdered sugar (depending on how sweet you want it)
1 teaspoon vanilla extract
1/4 - 1/2 cup graham cracker crumbs

Directions

Rinse strawberries and cut around the top of the strawberry. Remove the top and clean out with a paring knife, if necessary (some of them are hollow already.
Prepare all of the strawberries and set aside.
In a mixing bowl, beat cream cheese, powdered sugar, and vanilla until creamy. Add cream cheese mix to a piping bag or Ziploc with the corner snipped off.
Fill the strawberries with cheesecake mixture.
Once strawberries are filled, sprinkle or dip the tops with graham cracker crumbs. If not serving immediately, refrigerate until serving.

Nutritional Information
- Calories: 110.8
- Fat: 3.8 grams
- Carbohydrates: 14.1 grams
- Protein: 5.6 grams
- Fiber: 0.2 grams

Foods to Stay Away From when Eating Clean!

- **Any and all fast foods.** These are perhaps the worst offenders, as they somehow taste great when you are hungry, you eat them quickly, and they contain all the ingredients you don't need or your body wants; such as trans-fats, incorrect food combinations (cola drinks with proteins and carbohydrates), and an excess of calories.

- **Any "processed" food.** ANY... this means food that has been treated in an industrial setting.

- **An average fast food meal is about 1,000 or more calories.** It is often more, and leaves you hungry in about 2 hours.

- **Any "deep-fried" foods.** This includes the famous potato, but can also include fried meats (such as fried chicken), and some sweets, such as the donut or many oriental-type sweets. These kill your diet, raise insulin levels in the blood, and there is no way to lose weight.

- **All poly-saturated and animal fat.** We do not say to you to eliminate fat, just eat the correct ones. These are found in fish, some vegetables and some dairy products (where omega-3 oils have been incorporated to the dairy animal's feed).

- **White Flour.** There is nothing in it good for you, nothing. Whole wheat or other whole grains are another story. Eat them as you wish, but NO white flour. It is a dead food itself, and only causes unbalances in your digestive system. White flour was invented as it does not spoil, where whole grains do. The bugs know which is best to eat. They eat the whole grains and not bleached processed white flour.

- **White Sugar.** As its carbohydrate cousin above, white sugar also has very little or no nutritional value.

- There are so many healthy alternatives to it, and although sweet, these natural sugars are easily digested in your system as they are natural as you are natural.

- **Mayonnaise and its derivate.**
Although very tasty, and makes the food you eat it with so as well, the mayonnaise is heavily processed, usually with the cheapest oils, mostly trans fatty ones, and full of preservatives.

Clean Eating Principles

- Eating a mini-meal every two to three hours (5 to 6 small meals per day total) to keep blood sugar level and prevent hunger

- Combining lean proteins and complex carbs at every meal

- Avoiding all over-processed and refined foods (especially sugar, white rice, and white flour)

- Avoiding saturated and trans fat, instead consuming healthy fats

- Avoiding soda and other sugary juices and drinks

- Avoiding high-calorie, zero nutrient foods (i.e., junk food)

- Eating proper portion sizes

- Drinking at least 8 cups of water every day

Super Greens

Kale. You may have heard about kale recently, as it's quickly gaining in the ranks as one of the healthiest veggies you can eat, right up there with spinach. In fact in some areas it even outdoes spinach. Kale can be cooked and holds up to the heat much better than spinach, which ends up wilting and shrinking when cooked.

Benefits: The benefits of eating leafy greens like kale is that they contain phytonutrients, special antioxidants that help the body fend of things like inflammation, and basically make you feel better both now and over the long term if eaten consistently.

Spinach. Spinach is a superfood and is one of the best foods you can eat, no matter what diet you're on. It's packed with phytonutrients, fiber, extra minerals, and just plain helps the body. You'll be eating your fair share of meat on this diet so it's a good idea to pile on veggies like spinach to help with digestion and create a broad nutritional profile. Eat it fresh whenever you can, and frozen when you can't. Organic spinach is highly preferred over conventional since spinach leaves are very absorbent.

Benefits: The main benefits you're getting from spinach have to to be its anti-cancer benefits, as well as how it contributes to overall heart health so you're avoiding many types of heart disease. It contains a mix of antioxidants and phytonutrients that help battle the free radicals that enter the body from our modern lifestyle. It helps your overall well-being, gives you energy, and helps stabilize blood glucose levels.

Brocolli. Your mother probably told you to eat your broccoli, and as it turns out she was right on this one. It's a food that also ranks as one of the healthiest foods you can eat, period. It's also readily available year round, and you can find it fresh or frozen. There's almost always broccoli in the organic section of the produce department, and if there isn't there's usually an organic brand in the frozen veggies aisle.

Benefits: Perhaps the biggest reason to be eating broccoli is because its fiber content will help keep you regular. It's important to keep the digestive system moving because meat can fester in the intestines if you aren't getting enough fiber to help it along.

In addition to this the levels of Vitamin C are through the roof, and this is one of the most popular antioxidants that most know helps the immune system and can help you ward off colds and flus.

Cabbage. Although paler in color than other leafy greens, this cruciferous vegetable is a great source of cancer-fighting compounds and vitamin C. One of the most versatile greens "the workhorse of the kitchen."

Available in red and green varieties, cabbage can be cooked, added raw to salads or stir fries, shredded into a slaw, or made into sauerkraut.

It's also a staple of St. Patrick's Day boiled suppers and can give off a strong smell when cooking. One-half cup cooked has 15 calories.

What does a 1200 calorie day look like?

Your body uses calories each day to fuel itself. If you are attempting to lose weight, it's important to take in fewer calories than you expend. For many men and women, eating 1,200 calories a day provides the body with less fuel than it uses to operate. Typically, this means a net loss in weight.

If you are eating the right foods, you will not feel deprived and starving- High protein, complex carbs, and a high fiber diet is key!

I will display a typical 1200 calories day

Breakfast
3 egg whites
1/2 cup of oatmeal

Snack
Orange
10-12 Almonds

Lunch
4-6 oz of Fish on a salad with veggies

Snack
1 cup of celery
1 tablespoon of peanut butter

Dinner
4-6oz Grilled Chicken Breast
1/2 cup of couscous
1 cup of sautéed veggies

The principle behind weight loss is simple: you either have to burn more or eat fewer calories. It takes 3500 calories to lose 1 pound.

To lose weight, you need to create an energy (or calorie) deficit by eating fewer calories, increasing the number of calories you burn through physical activity, or both. 1200 calorie meal plans are typically safe without deprivation of important nutrients.

Always discuss a change in your diet or a new exercise program with your doctor.

SMOOTHIES AND JUICES

Why is juicing so important? Many benefits come from juicing and consuming fresh fruits and vegetables. Fruits and vegetables are filled with essential vitamins and minerals that are vital to curing or fighting many common disorders.

"The greatest wealth is Health!"

"Don't wish for it, work for it!"

Creamy Strawberry Blueberry Protein Smoothie (GF) (DF) (V)

This recipe was given to me by a good friend Kassy O'neal.. I love it!

Ingredients

1 Cup strawberries
1/2 cup blueberries
2 oranges juiced
1 lemon juiced

Handful of greens (spinach, kale etc.)
1/2 cup coconut milk
1/2 scoop protein powder (vanilla) - optional

Directions

I put my berries in the freezer the night before because I like my smoothie cold and it helps to not water it down with ice. Drop your berries, juice, greens and coconut milk into the blender. You can also add oats if you want more carbs but it's optional. Blend it really well especially if you added the oats to make sure the texture is nice, and then after everything is blended well add the protein powder (the protein powder is also optional but I add it for the extra vitamins and protein). Please keep in mind If you do add protein you need to drink immediately or it will thicken up a lot. The first time I made it I had a little science experiment unfolding on my desk after about 10 min. so I cut back to half a scoop and remembered not to forget it on my computer desk - smoothies are better chilly anyway. I love this recipe because you can add or subtract from the basic blend to suit your needs. I usually make a batch with coconut milk and a little vanilla protein powder and pour my portion into a glass then my husband uses the other half and adds oats cream and a little more protein powder for a more hefty version because he is trying to gain while I (like most women) am trying to slim up. You can also blend the basic version (berries, juice, greens, and coconut milk) and freeze it in an ice tray to use in the morning if you are in a hurry. Just get the smoothie cubes in the blender add coconut milk (or cream) oats, and a little protein powder (if wanted), blend, pour into a travel mug, and out the door you go.

Nutritional Information
- Calories: 220.1
- Fat: 6 grams
- Carbohydrates: 36.1 grams
- Protein: 14.7 grams
- Fiber: 2.8 grams

Berry and Spinach Smoothie

Start your morning off with a healthy juice!

Ingredients

1 cup(s) orange juice
1 cup(s) frozen blueberries
1/2 cup(s) frozen strawberries
1/2 cup(s) frozen raspberries
1 1/2 cup(s) loosely packed spinach
Honey or agave syrup, if necessary
Ice (optional)

Directions

Add the orange juice, fruit, and spinach to a blender.
Blend on medium-high speed until the all the spinach is blended and there are no visible green specks.
Add up to 2 tablespoons of agave syrup if necessary to sweeten.
Add additional ice cubes for an icier drink.

Nutritional Information
- Calories: 57.5
- Fat: 0.5 grams
- Carbohydrates: 5.7 grams
- Protein: 7.2 grams
- Fiber: 1.3 grams

Apple Pie Smoothie GF DF V

Ingredients

about 6 ice cubes
1 organic apple, washed, quartered and cored (leave the skin on)
1/2 frozen banana
1/2 C. unsweetened vanilla almond milk
1 t. cinnamon
pinch allspice

Directions

Put all ingredients, except for the stevia, into the blender.
Blend on high speed until smooth and creamy.
Add the stevia accordingly.

Nutritional Information
- Calories: 220.1
- Fat: 6 grams
- Carbohydrates: 36.1 grams
- Protein: 14.7 grams
- Fiber: 2.8 grams

Chocolate Avocado Smoothie

Ingredients

8 ounces almond milk
1/2 cup crushed ice
1 ripe banana
3 dates, or 1 tablespoon honey
1/2 avocado (about 1/4 cup)
2 tablespoons raw cacao
2 tablespoons almond butter
1 1/2 teaspoon golden flaxseed

Directions

Blend until smooth!

Nutritional Information
- Calories: 339.3
- Fat: 3.3 grams
- Carbohydrates: 44.3 grams
- Protein: 17.2 grams
- Fiber: 6.1 grams

Blueberry Blast GF DF V

Ingredients

1/2 cup of frozen blueberries
1/2 small banana
1/2 cucumber
1 tbsp of chia seeds
1 cup of water

Directions

Blend until smooth!

Nutritional Information
- Calories: 222.3
- Fat: 4 grams
- Carbohydrates: 30.5 grams
- Protein: 19 grams
- Fiber: 4 grams

Anti-Inflammatory Smoothie GF DF V

...to make your joints feel good!

Ingredients

1 stalk of celery
1 cup of cucumber
1/2 cup of pineapple
1/2 lime wedge
1 cup of coconut water

Directions

Blend until smooth!

Nutritional Information
- Calories: 138.3
- Fat: 0.7grams
- Carbohydrates: 34.9 grams
- Protein: 3.6 grams
- Fiber: 8.6 grams

Pineapple Avocado Smoothie

Ingredients

1 cup chopped pineapple (fresh or frozen)
1/2 large avocado
1 banana (fresh for frozen)
1/4 cup vanilla yogurt
1/3 cup almond or soy milk

Directions

Place all ingredients in a high speed blender.
If all your ingredients are fresh you may want to add 1/2 of ice to thicken the smoothie.
Blend all ingredients on high speed until smooth.
Pour in a glass and enjoy!

Nutritional Information
- Calories: 178.2
- Fat: 8.6 grams
- Carbohydrates: 27.8 grams
- Protein: 2.9 grams
- Fiber: 6.8 grams

Powerful Green Detox Juice

*This recipe is short and simple
and is packed with vitamins and nutrients!*

Ingredients

1 small Cucumber
1 small bunch Spinach
1 stalk Celery
1 small Apple or Pear

Directions

Juice all ingredients in a juicer and enjoy!

Nutritional Information
- Calories: 87.2
- Fat: 0.4 grams
- Carbohydrates: 11.6 grams
- Protein: 3.4 grams
- Fiber: 5.1 grams

Cindy's Green Juice ⓖⒻ ⓓⒻ Ⓥ

Want to feel energized? Try this juice for a pick me up!
Using my Nutri Bullet
Enjoy!

Ingredients

4-5 Ice cubes
Handful of spinach
Handful of kale
4-5 peeled baby carrots
1 tbsp of flax seed
1 large strawberry
1/2 cup of blueberries

Nutritional Information
- *Calories: 233.7*
- *Fat: 1.9 grams*
- *Carbohydrates: 59.9 grams*
- *Protein: 9.5 grams*
- *Fiber: 17.7 grams*

Carrot, Orange, Pineapple Juice GF DF V

A great detox juice

Ingredients

2 Carrots
1/4 Lemon, small
1 Orange, small
1/8 Pineapple, small rip

Nutritional Information
- Calories: 219.9
- Fat: 5.2 grams
- Carbohydrates: 43.9 grams
- Protein: 3.7 grams
- Fiber: 13.9 grams

Tropical Juice for Weight Loss

Not only will you feel you are in the Caribbean but you are fueling your body with key ingredients for metabolizing fat.

Ingredients

½ large pineapple
2 apples
16 oz. Alfalfa
16 oz. watercress
16 oz. parsley
16 oz. kale
16 oz. broccoli
2 oz. wheatgrass juice

Nutritional Information
- Calories: 253.2
- Fat: 2 grams
- Carbohydrates: 62.1 grams
- Protein: 4.4 grams
- Fiber: 8.5 grams

Artificial Sweeteners

They are in everything!

If you're trying to reduce the sugar and calories in your diet, you may be turning to artificial sweeteners or other sugar substitutes. You aren't alone. Today artificial sweeteners and other sugar substitutes are found in a variety of food and beverages marketed as "sugar-free" or "diet," including soft drinks, chewing gum, jellies, baked goods, candy, fruit juice, and ice cream and yogurt.

Just what are all these sweeteners? And what's their role in your diet?

Understanding artificial sweeteners and other sugar substitutes

Sugar substitutes are loosely considered any sweetener that you use instead of regular table sugar (sucrose). Artificial sweeteners are just one type of sugar substitute.

The chart lists some popular sugar substitutes and how they're commonly categorized.

The topic of sugar substitutes can be confusing. One problem is that the terminology is often open to interpretation.

For instance, some manufacturers call their sweeteners "natural" even though they're processed or refined, as is the case with stevia preparations. And some artificial sweeteners are derived from naturally occurring substances - sucralose comes from sugar, for example.

Regardless of how they're classified, sugar substitutes aren't magic bullets for weight loss. Take a closer look.

Artificial sweeteners	Sugar alcohols	Novel sweeteners	Natural sweeteners
Acesulfame potassium (Sunett, Sweet One)	Erythritol	Stevia extracts (Pure Via, Truvia)	Agave nectar
Aspartame (Equal, NutraSweet)	Hydrogenated starch hydrolysate	Tagatose (Naturlose)	Date sugar
Neotame	Isomalt	Trehalose	Fruit juice concentrate
Saccharin (SugarTwin, Sweet'N Low)	Lactitol		Honey
Sucralose (Splenda)	Maltitol		Maple syrup
	Mannitol		Molasses
	Sorbitol		
	Xylitol		

Artificial sweeteners

Artificial sweeteners are synthetic sugar substitutes but may be derived from naturally occurring substances, including herbs or sugar itself.

Artificial sweeteners are also known as intense sweeteners because they are many times sweeter than regular sugar.

Healthy Cooking Alternatives

SUBSTITUTIONS IN COOKING AND BAKING

Whipping up healthy recipes may be easier than you think. You can make simple ingredient substitutions to create healthy recipes that don't sacrifice taste and enjoyment.
Use this guide to help reduce the amount of fat, salt, sugar and calories as you prepare healthy recipes.

Your guide to ingredient substitutions for healthy recipes

If your recipe calls for this ingredient:	Try substituting this ingredient:
Bacon	Canadian bacon, turkey bacon, smoked turkey or lean prosciutto (Italian ham)
Bread, white	Whole-grain bread
Bread crumbs, dry	Rolled oats or crushed bran cereal
Butter, margarine, shortening or oil in baked goods	Applesauce or prune puree for half of the called-for butter, shortening or oil; butter spreads or shortenings specially formulated for baking that don't have trans fats. *Note:* To avoid dense, soggy or flat baked goods, don't substitute oil for butter or shortening. Also don't substitute diet, whipped or tub-style margarine for regular margarine.
Butter, margarine, shortening or oil to prevent sticking	Cooking spray or nonstick pans
Cream	Fat-free half-and-half, evaporated skim milk

Cream cheese, full fat	Fat-free or low-fat cream cheese, Neufchatel, or low-fat cottage cheese pureed until smooth.
Eggs	Two egg whites or 1/4 cup egg substitute for each whole egg.
	Whole-wheat flour for half of the called-for all-purpose flour in baked goods *Note:* Whole-wheat pastry flour is less dense and works well in softer products like cakes and muffins.
Fruit canned in heavy syrup	Fruit canned in its own juices or in water, or fresh fruit
Ground beef	Extra-lean or lean ground beef, chicken or turkey breast (make sure no poultry skin has been added to the product)
Lettuce, iceberg	Arugula, chicory, collard greens, dandelion greens, kale, mustard greens, spinach or watercress.
Mayonnaise	Reduced-calorie mayonnaise-type salad dressing or reduced-calorie, reduced-fat mayonnaise.
Meat as the main ingredient	Three times as many vegetables as the meat on pizzas or in casseroles, soups and stews.
Milk, evaporated	Evaporated skim milk.
Milk, whole	Reduced-fat or fat-free milk.
Oil-based marinades	Wine, balsamic vinegar, fruit juice or fat-free broth.
Pasta, enriched (white)	Whole-wheat pasta.
Rice, white	Brown rice, wild rice, bulgur or pearl barley.
Salad dressing	Fat-free or reduced-calorie dressing or flavored vinegars.
Seasoning salt, such as garlic salt, celery salt or onion salt	Herb-only seasonings, such as garlic powder, celery seed or onion flakes, or use finely chopped herbs or garlic, celery or onions.
Soups, creamed	Fat-free milk-based soups, mashed potato flakes, or pureed carrots, potatoes or tofu for thickening agents.
Soups, sauces, dressings, crackers, or canned meat, fish or vegetables	Low-sodium or reduced-sodium versions

Sour cream, full fat	Fat-free or low-fat sour cream, plain fat-free or low-fat yogurt.
Soy sauce	Sweet-and-sour sauce, hot mustard sauce or low-sodium soy sauce.
Sugar	In most baked goods you can reduce the amount of sugar by one-half; intensify sweetness by adding vanilla, nutmeg or cinnamon.
Syrup	Pureed fruit, such as applesauce, or low-calorie, sugar-free syrup.
Table salt	Herbs, spices, citrus juices (lemon, lime, orange), rice vinegar, salt-free seasoning mixes or herb blends.
Yogurt, fruit-flavored	Plain yogurt with fresh fruit slices.

DRESSING AND SAUCES

"A year from now you will wish you had started today."
Karen Lamb

"Excuses don't burn calories."

Ranch dressing recipe

Ingredients

1/2 cup of plain Greek yogurt
1/3 cup of real mayo- olive oil blend
1/3-1/2 cup of almond milk (depending on how thick you want it)
1/2 tsp of garlic powder
1/2 tsp onion powder
1/2 tsp of sea salt
1/2 tsp of pepper
1/2 tsp of chopped green onions
1 tsp of parsley flakes (dried or fresh)
1/2 tsp dill (dried or fresh)

Directions

Mix together and refrigerate. *Enjoy!*

Nutritional Information
- Calories: 17.5
- Fat: 0.1 grams
- Carbohydrates: 1.1 grams
- Protein: 2.6 grams
- Fiber: 0.5 grams

Pesto GF DF V

Ingredients

1 tablespoon olive oil
3 tablespoons Dijon mustard
2 tablespoons honey (called for maple syrup)

1 tablespoon minced fresh sage leaves
1/4 teaspoon salt
1/8 teaspoon pepper
2 small sweet potatoes, peeled, cut into 1/4 - inch thick disks
Cooking spray

Directions

Mix together and refrigerate. *Enjoy!*

Nutritional Information
- Calories: 63.9
- Fat: 6.7 grams
- Carbohydrates: 0.5 grams
- Protein: 0.8 grams
- Fiber: 0.2 grams

Avocado Relish GF DF V

Ingredients

1 small avocado, peeled, seeded and finely chopped
1/2 cup coarsely chopped tomato
1/4 cup finely chopped red onion
2 tablespoons chopped fresh cilantro
2 tablespoons olive oil
1 tablespoon lime juice
1/2 tablespoon Red Pepper, Crushed
1/8 teaspoon Sea Salt

Nutritional Information
- Calories: 166.7
- Fat: 14.8 grams
- Carbohydrates: 10.1 grams
- Protein: 2.2 grams
- Fiber: 6.9 grams

Zucchini- Avocado Salsa

This salsa is wonderful on just about any dish!

Ingredients

1 Zucchini
1/2 cup of fresh cilantro, chopped
1/4 cup of red onion
Zest from 1 lime and juice from 2 limes
1/2 teaspoon of honey
1 small avocado, diced
sea salt & pepper to taste

Directions

Puree all in a food processor except for avocado.
Stir in diced avocado, spread over fish.

Nutritional Information
- Calories: 180
- Fat: 13.8 grams
- Carbohydrates: 15.4 grams
- Protein: 3.2 grams
- Fiber: 8 grams

Chicken Shawarma Sauce

Ingredients

1/2 cupplain 2% reduced-fat Greek yogurt
2 tablespoons tahini
2 teaspoons fresh lemon juice
1/4 teaspoon salt
1 garlic clove, minced

Directions

In a food processor, blend all ingredients together until smooth.

Nutritional Information
- Calories: 242.5
- Fat: 9.1 grams
- Carbohydrates: 14.6 grams
- Protein: 25.6 grams
- Fiber: 1.8 grams

Holiday Shrimp Cocktail GF DF V

Sauce Ingredients

1 cup ketchup
1 Lemon juiced
1 teaspoon of Worcestershire sauce
1/2 teaspoon sea salt
1/2 teaspoon fresh ground pepper

Directions

Whisk all ingredients together in a small bowl.

Nutritional Information
- Calories: 44.9
- Fat: 0 grams
- Carbohydrates: 11.9 grams
- Protein: 0.5 grams
- Fiber: 0.3 grams

Lemon Mint Sauce (GF) (DF) (V)

This is a light and tasty sauce that you can pair with fish, chicken, or salads.

Ingredients

1 tablespoon fresh mint chopped
1/3 cup of olive oil
1 lemon
1 tsp of fresh ground pepper
1 tsp of sea salt
1 packet of stevia

Directions

In a small bowl pour 1/3 cup of olive oil.
1 tsp of lemon zest. 2 tbsp of lemon juice.
Add the mint, pepper, sea salt, stevia and set to the side.

Nutritional Information
- Calories: 56
- Fat: 1.5 grams
- Carbohydrates: 3.4 grams
- Protein: 0.6 grams
- Fiber: 0.5 grams

Creamy Tomato Sauce

Ingredients

20 cherry tomatoes
2 cloves of garlic
2 tablespoons of tahini
3 teaspoons of dried basil
1 teaspoon oregano
1 teaspoon sea salt
1 teaspoon ground black pepper

Directions

Add all ingredients into a food processor, blend until smooth.

Nutritional Information
- Calories: 89
- Fat: 4.9 grams
- Carbohydrates: 15.4 grams
- Protein: 0.5 grams
- Fiber: 2.4 grams

Berries are Superfoods that can improve your overall health!

Berries are a nutri-rich food that help with the dreaded term, aging!

Listed below are the benefits to the tasty fruits, enjoy, and improve your health at the same time!

Blackberries

They are special, beyond their basic berry goodness.

Notable for their high levels of dietary fiber, vitamin C, vitamin K, folic acid and manganese, they also rank well for antioxidant strength, with notable levels of polyphenolic compounds, such as ellagic acid, tannins, ellagitannins, quercetin, gallic acid, anthocyanins and cyanidins. By many accounts, blackberries are considered one of the strongest antioxidant foods consumed in the U.S.

Blueberries

Second only to strawberries in terms of U.S. berry consumption, blueberries are not only popular, but constantly rank near the top in terms of their antioxidant capacities among all fruits, vegetables, spices and seasonings.

Studies suggest that blueberries may reduce memory decline, may reduce heart attack risk, and may provide other anti-aging benefits. They are also an excellent source of vitamins C and K, manganese and a good source of dietary fiber.

One of the real beauties of blueberries is that they are native to North America and are grown commercially in 38 states, meaning fewer food miles and habitat destruction than some of their superfood sisters. Unfortunately, domestic blueberries test positive for 42 different pesticide residues in EWG's examination of pesticide loads – so purchase organic ones when you can.

Raspberries

The U.S. is the third-largest raspberry producer in the world, which is a good thing given our fondness for them and the health benefits they deliver. Because of their aggregate fruit structure, raspberries are among the highest fiber-containing foods, with up to 20 percent fiber per total weight. They are also a great source of vitamin C, manganese, B vitamins 1–3, folic acid, magnesium, copper and iron. As for the antioxidants, raspberries contain the all-important anthocyanins, ellagic acid, quercetin, gallic acid, cyanidins, pelargonidins, catechins, kaempferol and salicylic acid. Yellow raspberries are also grown, but they have fewer antioxidants.

A compound found in raspberries, raspberry ketone, is routinely touted as a weight loss supplement, though more research is needed to determine the veracity of the claims.

Strawberries

Although strawberries are grown in every state in the U.S., California manages to grow 75 percent of the nation's crops – in fact, the Golden State produces more than 1 billion pounds of strawberries a year, which is surely appreciated by the 94 percent of U.S. households that consume the sweet red berries.

Although strawberries aren't exotic and don't require long traveling distances and dwindling rain forests to thrive, they are one of the stellar powerhouses of the berry group.

One serving of strawberries offers 85 milligrams of vitamin C, or 150 percent of the Daily Value.

They provide fiber, manganese, folate, potassium, and like the rest of the berry family, antioxidants. Strawberries land in second place for pesticide load on EWG's 2013 Dirty Dozen list, so purchase organic ones if you can.

Benefits of Dark Chocolate

Dark Chocolate is Very Nutritious

If you buy quality dark chocolate with a high cocoa content, then it is actually quite nutritious.

It contains a decent amount of soluble fiber and is loaded with minerals.

A 100 gram bar of dark chocolate with 70-85% cocoa contains (1):
- *11 grams of fiber.*
- *67% of the RDA for Iron.*
- *58% of the RDA for Magnesium.*
- *89% of the RDA for Copper.*
- *98% of the RDA for Manganese.*
- *It also has plenty of potassium, phosphorus, zinc and selenium.*

Dark Chocolate is a Powerful Source of Antioxidants

Dark Chocolate May Improve Blood Flow and Lower Blood Pressure

Dark Chocolate Raises HDL and Protects LDL Against Oxidation

Dark Chocolate May Lower The Risk of Cardiovascular Disease

Dark Chocolate May Protect Your Skin Against The Sun

Dark Chocolate May Improve Brain Function

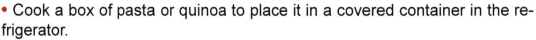

PREPARING MEALS

• Cook a box of pasta or quinoa to place it in a covered container in the refrigerator.
Then you could use the pasta later in the week for Pistachio Pesto Pasta or use the quinoa to make Quinoa Protein Bars or Grilled Vegetables and Quinoa.

• Hard-boil some eggs for breakfast, snack, or to use in egg salad sandwiches.

• Grill chicken and vegetables and place them in a covered container to use throughout the week for wraps, pasta, or quesadillas.

• Grill chicken and vegetables and place them in a covered container to use throughout the week for wraps, pasta, or quesadillas.

• Soups are great to make ahead, and you can always freeze whatever you have leftover so make a double batch!

• Homemade pesto and hummus are two things I've starting making recently. I can't believe I never made before but now that I do I can't go back to store bought. They take minutes and it's all done in the food processor! Then I can use them on wraps, pasta, dipping sauces, and salads.

- Muesli is great and easy to make- also can be put in Mason jars.

- Make a couple days' worth of school lunches on Sunday night. It'll save you so much trouble throughout the week if you take care of two – three days at once!make a double batch!

- Mason jars salads will help you get a healthy lunch that is ready to go and is already packed to take to work for the week. They will stay good for four to five days in the refrigerator and take just a few minutes to make, especially if you took the time to clean and chop off the vegetables.

- Mason Jar Yogurt Parfaits are great for breakfast, or pack them to take with you for lunch.

Omega 3's and how do you get them from food

- Omega-3 is a high-profile nutritional trend, ranking alongside with calcium and fiber in consumers' concerns [source: Watson]. And unlike some food fads that are over in a flash, the need for omega-3 may be as genuine as advertised.
- Omega-3 refers to omega-3 fatty acids. Fatty acids are the building blocks of fats, which, despite their misunderstood reputation, are vital nutrients. Omega-3 is used to regulate blood clotting, build cell membranes and support cell health. It's polyunsaturated, which is the relatively heart-healthy kind of fats that help reduce blood triglycerides (fats) and low-density lipoprotein (LDL), the so-called bad cholesterol.
- Omega-3 also curbs inflammation. While inflammation is a normal part of the body's immune response, research indicates that it also underlies a host of serious illnesses, including cardiovascular diseases, cancers and autoimmune diseases.
- Omega-3 is called an essential fatty acid: It's essential to health, and because the human body doesn't produce it, it's essential in the diet. Unfortunately, the typical American diet includes relatively few foods that are rich in omega-3.

SHOPPING FOR OMEGA-3 FATTY ACIDS

- Ready to get more omega-3 fatty acids in your diet? We've put together this quick shopping list to take along the next time you go to the supermarket.

FISH: TOP SOURCE OF OMEGA-3 FATTY ACIDS

• Seafood is a great source for DHA and EPA omega-3s, both essential for healthy hearts and brains. Look for seafood rich in omega-3s, such as:

- Halibut
- Herring
- Mackerel
- Oysters
- Salmon
- Sardines
- Trout
- Tuna (fresh)

THE COLD CASE: FORTIFIED DAIRY, JUICES

• Functional foods are defined as any food that provides health benefits beyond basic nutrition. These days, supermarkets are brimming with foods enhanced with omega-3s, from fortified juice to eggs produced by chickens fed omega-3s in their grain. You'll likely find the following foods fortified with omega-3 fatty acids:

- Eggs
- Margarine
- Milk
- Juice
- Soy milk
- Yogurt

GRAINS AND NUTS WITH OMEGA-3S

• Bread and pasta are some of the foods most commonly enriched with omega-3s. You'll also find them in whole foods like seeds and nuts. When shopping, look for omega-3s in:

- Bread
- Cereal
- Crunchy Oats
- Flaxseed
- Flour
- Pasta
- Peanut butter
- Oatmeal
- Pumpkin seeds
- Pizza, packaged
- Flour tortillas
- Walnuts

FRESH PRODUCE WITH ALA OMEGA-3S

- Vegetables, especially green leafy ones, are rich in ALA, one form of omega-3 fatty acids. Although ALA isn't as powerful as the other omega-3 fatty acids, DHA and EPA, these vegetables offer a host of benefits, from fiber to antioxidants, in addition to omega-3.
    - Brussels sprouts
    - Kale
    - Mint
    - Parsley
    - Spinach
    - Watercress

Oil with ALA Omega-3s

- Oils can be a good source of ALA omega-3s, too, including:
    - Rapeseed oil
    - Cod liver oil
    - Flaxseed oil
    - Mustard oil
    - Soybean oil
    - Walnut oil

Lettuce – Which one do we choose and which one is the best for us and why?

- As the USDA database and our abbreviated table make clear, not all lettuces are created equal. Iceberg lettuce, which is by far the most popular lettuce in the United States, delivers the least nutritional bang for the buck. Although it has more fiber than some lettuces, it's a bit of a dud when it comes to vitamin and mineral content. And it's high in sugar, which is a major source of calories.

- Romaine lettuce is a better choice. Romaine has less sugar and more fiber. But it really excels in the vitamin and mineral departments. It's an excellent source of vitamin C and a good source of folate and vitamin A. It also provides 10 times more beta carotene than iceberg lettuce and almost as much as spinach. All of this combines to make romaine one of the healthiest of all the lettuces.

- Green-leaf lettuce is a solid runner-up. It's low in fat and sugar and high in protein. It also delivers decent amounts of calcium, phosphorous, potassium, manganese and vitamins C, A and K. Red-leaf and butterhead lettuces aren't slouches either, as they surpass iceberg varieties in almost every nutrient category and have the highest amount of iron of all lettuces.

- So if you really want to stay strong to the finish, stick with romaine and the other dark green leafy lettuces while cutting back on the crispheads. And don't forget to spice things up with the more exotic members of the family, such as arugula, curly endive, escarole and radicchio.

Key Nutrients in Lettuce

Source: USDA National Nutrient Database for Standard Reference ©2010 HowStuffWorks

NUTRIENT	VALUE (per cup of shredded lettuce)				
	LOOSE LEAF				
	Red Leaf	Green Leaf	Romaine	Iceberg	Butterhead
Water	26.78 g	34.23 g	44.47 g	68.86 g	52.60 g
Protein	0.37 g	0.49 g	0.58 g	0.65 g	0.74 g
Total lipid (fat)	0.06 g	0.05 g	0.14 g	0.10 g	0.12 g
Fiber, total dietary	0.3 g	0.5 g	1.0 g	0.9 g	0.6 g
Sugars, total	0.13 g	0.28 g	0.56 g	1.42 g	0.52 g
SELECTED MINERALS					
Calcium, Ca	9 mg	13 mg	16 mg	13 mg	19 mg
Iron, Fe	0.34 mg	0.31 mg	0.46 mg	0.30 mg	0.68 mg
Magnesium, Mg	3 mg	5 mg	7 mg	5 mg	7 mg
Potassium, K	52 mg	70 mg	116 mg	102 mg	131 mg
Sodium, Na	7 mg	10 mg	4 mg	7 mg	3 mg
SELECTED VITAMINS					
Vitamin C	1.0 mg	6.5 mg	11.3 mg	2 mg	2.0 mg
Vitamin A	0.105 mg	0.133 mg	0.205 mg	0.018 mg	0.091 mg
Riboflavin	0.022 mg	0.029 mg	0.031 mg	0.018 mg	0.034 mg
Niacin	0.090 mg	0.135 mg	0.147 mg	0.089 mg	0.196 mg
Folate	0.010 mg	0.014 mg	0.064 mg	0.021 mg	0.040 mg
Vitamin K	0.0393 mg	0.0625 mg	0.0482 mg	0.0174 mg	0.0563 mg

Acknowledgement

Over the years Bodies By Cindy has become a family and a small community, and I am honored to be a part of it. Thanks to each and every one of my clients who share their stores with me- their ups, their downs, their setbacks, and their accomplishments. It drives me to want to be a better person and motivated me to create the Fat to Fit with Cindy Lane Ross line. Working with all of you is a passion of mine and truly makes my heart happy knowing that I have helped you achieve a better quality of life.

People always asks me, "Cindy, what motivates you to work so much?" First of all when you love what you do, it isn't work but when my mom died in 2006, something changed inside of me and I knew my mission was to help people. For so many years I was undecided on my future, but the day my mom died, I knew I wanted to help people achieve a better quality of life. Life is too short to sit on the sidelines, believe me I know from my own experience. It's not about whether or not you have a "six pack", it's about how you feel and having enough energy to enjoy the rest of the days of your life.

There is a power greater than myself that motivates me to help people change their lives. Thank you to everyone in my life for all the encouragement you have given me. I love you all more than words can express! I wish my mom was alive to see my first cookbook published, I think she might have been amazed since I had no clue about cooking growing up!

Writing this book has brought me great pleasure in knowing that I am teaching you to lead a better quality of life and with hopes you will pass it on to those around you.

"Live each day as if it was your last!"

XOXO

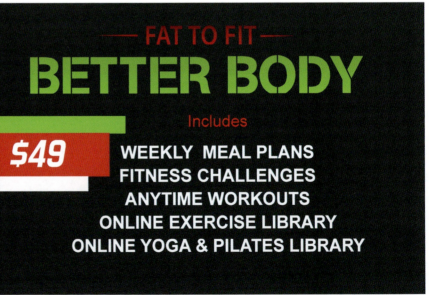

FAT TO FIT
3 Month Makeover

Includes

MEAL PLANS
GROCERY LIST
TRAINING SCHEDULE
TRAINING REGIMEN
WEEKLY HITT WORKOUTS

$150

FAT TO FIT
JUMPSTART

Includes

YOGA & PILATES LIBRARY
WORKOUT TRACKERS
ONLINE EXERCISE LIBRARY

$99

Made in the USA
Charleston, SC
04 June 2015